God's Fingerprints Everywhere

Heart of Mary

AUTHOR MARY MARTIN

May you draw closer
to God through this
book.
Love Mary

God's Fingeprints Everywhere

MARY MARTIN

A Devotional Memoir

Kindle Direct Publishing

First printed in the United Kingdom by Kindle Direct Publishing

First Printing, 2024

ISBN [978-1-7384856-1-1]

God's fingerprints everywhere

Contents in Chronological order

(In every country, God guides, provides, protects, understands, and reveals. To read the stories in subject order, there is a list with page numbers at the back of the book.)

New Zealand 6-19yrs

Australia 1984

England 2013 – 2023

Tablet of Contents by Subjetcs

God who Guides.

God who Provides.

God who protects.

God who understands.

God reveals Himself.

Preface

I'm the last person in the world who ever thought they'd write a book. Until last year, you could count the number of books I had read on one hand.

The writing part reminded me of school, and school was no picnic. Early in school, I was left at the back of the classroom as though I was stupid, so I thought that must be true. The classes in primary school were so big that the teachers seemed to choose the clever kids and teach them while the rest of us spent most of the day coloring pictures.

When I was nine, the class was smaller, and the teacher noticed me. She seemed to want me to learn, so I went to a reading recovery class, but due to also being dyslexic, I didn't have a clue how to read. My mother loved reading, but I preferred acting out stories with friends.

So, it was a huge surprise to me in 2020, when the world closed down and I thought about recording stories from my life for my son. I had him at 42 years old and realised he knew nothing of my "God stories" world travels. I also knew so little about how to write a book and happened across a Facebook Writers Learning Together group. I joined, feeling like a fraud, and was encouraged to keep writing.

God also decided to get involved in this project and soon reminded me of many great memories He wanted to tell others.

Ninety stories later, I've written a book—God's Fingerprints Everywhere. Through saying YES so long ago to God and following Him around the world, serving others regardless of education, status, ethnicity, age, gender, or family background, I discovered that God could work through me to tell His story.

Come along with me and find out what God and I have done together, and be open to it affecting your life as well.

—Mary Martin
Spring 2024

I'm Not Looking Like Much

Before I formed you in the womb I knew you,
before you were born, I set you apart.
Jeremiah 1:5

I dreaded the teacher's opinion of me. It was parent's interview time at primary school again. School was never easy for me. I was deaf until I was seven years old from continual ear infections; I would lip-read the teachers, and I was always in trouble for not hearing them when they told us to pay attention. Added to this, I was dyslexic. I always felt either I had no idea what was happening, or the teacher didn't care about helping me understand it. When I was eight years old, I decided school was only for eating your lunch with your friends and playing. After all, I believed teachers were only ever interested in clever kids.

It was finally my mother's turn to hear how I was doing from my teacher. My mother asked sprightly, "How is my daughter Mary doing?"

Not even taking a moment to consider my strengths, the teacher replied, "She'll probably make a lovely housewife," conveying there wasn't much hope that I would do much else with my life.

The following day at school, not knowing my mother had told me what the teacher had said, the teacher came over to me and asked me, "What are you going to be when you grow up?"

I loudly and casually proclaimed, "I'm going to do something for God." She rolled her eyes back and smirked as she walked away, but I knew I would do that one day. I promptly got back to bossing my friends around as I directed our acting game.

After completing my nursing training, I remembered what I had said to the teacher, and it made sense why I was now preparing to go to the Philippines to work as a nurse in a free clinic.

I was now twenty years old and being sent from my church to the Philippines in a dedicated service. The teacher who had asked me that question attended my church. She approached me and reminded me of what I had said I would do as a nine-year-old. The memory came back. The word God had put in my heart as a young child meant even if the teachers didn't see potential in me, God did; and God took the time to put that in my mind even as a child.

Reflection:

1. Did God ever give you a sense of your future as a child, or anything else of importance? If you are seeking guidance, ask God to remind you of things He has impressed on your heart.
2. Have you done any of those things yet? Or do you still need to fulfil them? God is patient and kind, and you can always do what God has asked you to do.

I Didn't Wanted To Be Left Behind

Do not let your hearts be troubled. You believe in God; believe also in me. My Father's house has many rooms; if that were not so, would I have told you that I am going there to prepare a place for you? And if I go and prepare a place for you, I will come back and take you to be with me so that you also may be where I am.
John 14:1–3

It was early spring, and the drafty old church made it feel bitterly cold. It was time to go to Sunday school. I wasn't going to take my coat off in that hall like the other kids were doing. Growing up in New Zealand without central heating meant our homes and buildings were icy cold. The crazy pioneer spirit meant we had to be tough. We even had to sing swift action songs to help keep us warmed up.

Now, it was time to sit still to listen to the message, which I thought came directly from God through this very tall man, who was much closer to heaven than I was. To a six-year-old, he seemed as authoritative as my maths teacher—as though he knew what he was talking about. Despite the cold room, I wanted to hear more.

He said, "Jesus is coming back to get us, and we don't want to be left behind."

I did not want to be left behind by anyone. I felt a bit scared, but I still wanted to hear more. I leaned my body forward to listen to what I needed to do so I wouldn't be left behind.

"Believe in Jesus," he said, "that He came from God to earth, and ask Him to forgive you, and you won't be left behind."

I couldn't get that out of my mind, and I couldn't get home fast enough. I knelt by my bed and asked Jesus to forgive me for all the bad things I had done and for Him to become the boss of my life. I liked being in charge of my friends, so I knew what boss meant.

I looked around, thinking maybe an angel or at least a flash of lightning would appear, but that didn't happen. It was just me and my dolls in the room. Somehow, I knew I belonged to God now, and He would tell me what to do like someone in charge does. I left my room, went to my mother (who was doing the dishes), and told her what I had done. I had a new friend who would not leave me behind.

Reflection:

1. Are you ready for when Jesus comes back for those who believed in Him?

Auntie Peggy's Shoes

Jesus said, "Let the little children come to me, and do not hinder them, for the kingdom of heaven belongs to such as these."
Matthew 19:14

"Size five shoes!" I exclaimed. "Wow, they are beautiful." I'd never seen feet that small. My auntie, my father's sister, had just arrived from England, and I was eight years old. My mother had size nine feet, so I assumed and dreaded that I would end up with feet like hers.

I was eager to get on my knees that night and pray. I knew exactly what I was going to ask the Lord for.

I knelt at my bed and said, "Lord, ignore all other prayer requests I've made; I just want You to grant me size five feet when I'm all grown up."

I wasn't sure one prayer was enough, so I prayed seven nights, every night that Auntie was with us.

Auntie was so dainty and feminine with beautiful clothes, just like in the movies. My mother didn't care about fashion; she was efficient and liked warmth over style. One time, when Mum couldn't find a woolen hat, she put a tea cosy on her head.

But I was also related to this woman on my father's side, so it could happen. God was more than able to answer this prayer. (Well, it was at least worth a try.)

It also stirred a desire to travel to England, where Auntie had come from. One day, I would eventually go to England, and God must have smiled when I asked for size five feet, because this happened, too.

Reflection:

1. It is essential to encourage our children to pray and see that God is a God who can answer prayers, including our desires.
2. Does my faith as a child encourage you? As I recorded the story, it inspired me to have more childlike faith, as I did then.

Taken Away

For the Lord God is a sun and shield; the Lord bestows favour and honour; no good thing does he withhold from those whose walk is blameless.
Psalm 84:11

My mother fostered children. When I was three years old, Danny came to live with us. I thought of him as a brother. He was born with a condition called hydrocephalus, which gave him a large head. I didn't notice anything. I simply loved him.

Two years later, a lady came to the door to get him, and as quickly as he appeared, he was gone. I didn't understand. I ran to my mother's room. She was on the bed weeping.

"Mum!" I yelled. "Go after her. How can you let her take him? Get up and bring him back! He's my brother; we are family!"

I ran out of the house and down our long driveway, screaming, "Whoever you are, bring him back NOW!" I fell in a heap on the pavement, pounding my fists and crying. "Mum, do something," I kept saying.

Why was he taken? Would a strange lady come one day and take me away? In my anxiousness, my mother calmly bent down to my level and said, "It was time for him to go."

Whatever did she mean? I thought she was mean and cruel, and it put a wedge between me and Mum for years (not that I understood that then).

It wasn't till I grew up and found a photo of Danny that I brought the subject up again. My mother explained that his mother had always wanted him back but needed to work through her issues. Social welfare said she was now ready to be a mother again. I partly understood, but it left an untruth in my heart: "good things get taken away."

Years later, when I was in a relationship and learning to trust God more with my future, I had an unwarranted fear that my boyfriend would have to leave me. In my daily reading, I read Psalm 84:11. A deep peace came over me. I could trust God to care for me. I also felt God's comfort for the pain of Danny leaving.

Reflection:

1. Can you identify with something precious being taken from you?
2. How did it make you feel?
3. Can you see God in this story? Can you invite Him into your pain?

God Knows How to Communicate with Us

So Eli told Samuel, "Go and lie down, and if he calls you, say, 'Speak, Lord, for your servant is listening.'"
1 Samuel 3:9

I did not know who C. S. Lewis was, nor his books on Narnia and the Wardrobe, because I never read anything as a child. Why would I even try? No one at school believed I could read or understand the written word, so I didn't even bother. I had a good imagination, so I made up stories and made my friends act them out.

My bedroom had an extended, dark, built-in wardrobe, which seemed endless. I would imagine all kinds of things as we went on our adventures to faraway lands.

One particular day, as I was playing with a friend, going in and out of my wardrobe, I stopped and announced boldly and with deep conviction, "One day, I'm going to the other side of this wardrobe in Germany, and it's snowing there."

It was so random. I didn't even know where Germany was or that it snowed there.

Little did I know then that I was speaking a prophetic word over my life. In 1990, I would fulfil this word by going to share my faith in East Germany after the Berlin Wall had come down. Once I got off the plane in Frankfurt, the memory of my ten-year-old self returned to me.

Reflection:

1. Does this story help you to see that even with our limitations, we can trust God to lead us like Samuel in the story above? He was learning to discern who was guiding him.

Life Can Be Short

He will respond to the prayer of the destitute; he will not despise their plea.
Psalm 102:17

We were the last ones to see him alive. I was ten years old, staying the weekend with a school friend, happily playing dress-up, when her brother entered the lounge. He proceeded to say, "Goodbye," in a prolonged and loving way. I'd never heard him speak like this before.

Not understanding why he was using this tone to say goodbye, I responded without much thought: "Bye."

The following day, two policemen stood at my friend's front door. We opened the door, and they asked to speak to the mother or father of the house. Her mother came. We hurried off to another room to play, but then I heard the belly cry of a mother in distress roaring out—NO . . . It was like no other sound I had ever heard. We still had no idea what had happened but assumed it was terrible news. My friend was called in and told that her brother had ended his life. He had been found in his car at a rubbish dump, having gassed himself from the fumes of the car. Suddenly, everything seemed dark, like the sun had disappeared, and a deep sadness descended over the entire house.

My friend did not cry or say anything; she was in shock. She just wanted to get out of the house immediately. We strolled along to my house, not

too many nightmares of his face saying goodbye and visions of his coffin. My friend's mother never seemed to be the same after this.
There are some things we never get entirely over, but later in life, I did learn to talk to God about things I didn't understand.

Reflection:
1. Where was God in this?
2. How are we meant to cope with suffering (especially when there is no way to understand it or provide someone with a good reason for why it happened)?
3. If you've never talked to God about some deep questions, know it's okay to do so. David complains to God in the Psalms. He's honest about his situation, but if you read the whole psalm, you see how he sees God at the end.

Whatever You Do, God Is There

He will respond to the prayer of the destitute; he will not despise their plea.
Psalm 102:17

I was so excited. I was allowed to stay over on a Saturday night with my new friend from school. I only ever went to church on the weekends on Sundays, so this was huge. She wasn't from a Christian family, so she didn't go to church. I was even allowed to ride my bike there, but I had to be back for the 11 am church service the following day.

I was eleven and a half years old and didn't want to attend church anymore. That was for children, not me. I was nearly a teenager. But attending church had been the only condition I was allowed to go to my friend's house at all. My mother said, "We have to go to church every Sunday unless we are dying." Only older people died, so I figured that meant I'd be going for a long time. So, what did it matter if I missed one?

We had a fun evening doing many silly things and hardly slept. Morning came, and I had to go to church, of course. I got on my bike in a very agitated way. It wasn't fair that I had to be the first of my friends to leave. They had planned to ride the horses that morning. That sounded much more fun than attending church to listen to older men praying for ages, other men snoring, and my mother tapping me to stay still.

I biked as hard as I could. I was angry. Why did other kids get to have fun on Sundays?

In this frenzy, I felt God's eyes on me. He seemed like this big, mean God who decided I would be born into a family that played by the rules. I looked up to the sky and said, "Stop watching me. I want to enjoy my life."

Reflection:
1. How did you view God as a child?
2. Do you still think of God in that way?
3. Do you believe God wants you to enjoy your life?

His Love Breaks Through

How priceless is your unfailing love, O God! People take refuge in the shadow of your wings.
Psalm 36:7

I was so bored. It was the church's Annual General Meeting, and Dad was at work, so I had to attend this tedious, long meeting with Mum. I wasn't interested in the old religion of rules and long prayers. I went to sit on the steps outside the church to wait for Mum.

It was a lovely, warm Saturday evening, which made matters worse, as I should have been with friends my age. I was thirteen years old but attended a church full of older adults and young families.

As I was sulking over this, a car pulled up, driven by a guy in his late teens. I recognised him from a church youth event. He rolled down his window and said, "Do you want a ride to the church youth group tonight?" These steps seemed to be the meeting place for a ride. While he waited for more teenagers to arrive, I ran to my mother to ask her if I could go. She knew the couple who ran it, so she said yes.

There was something different about this group of Christian teenagers. I felt the love of God like never before. I felt so welcome. We could hardly fit in the room, as there were so many of us. They sang worship songs—new to me—and prayed. I had only heard very long prayers from much older men. But here, anyone could pray, even girls, and short prayers were encouraged. It didn't matter how well-educated or articulate you were. We were all the same, no matter what our background was. All were welcome, and suddenly, I had a group where I belonged. I watched and wanted to cry as God's love was almost tangible.

Reflection:
1. Do you think God pursues us, even when we show no interest in Him?
2. Have you experienced His love for you? I believe He so longs to show you this.

The Camp That Changed My Life

At that time Jesus came from Nazareth in Galilee and was baptised by John in river Jordan.
Mark 1:9

I was still on the edge, watching everyone. I hadn't grown up with siblings, as my two brothers were older than me and left home when I was ten. There weren't any families with kids my age on my street. I didn't go anywhere except church on Sunday.

I was timid, awkward, and struggling with my appearance, due to acne. The boys in the youth group were going camping, so three lady leaders decided to plan a "girls' getaway." These ladies made me feel welcome and included in all activities. Watching their lives, I knew I was a long way from God.

We had a lot of fun doing activities inside and outside, including Bible study. During one of the Bible study sessions, I felt so unworthy and ran crying back to my bunk room. One of the leaders came in, and I told her how I felt. It was the first time I had shared my innermost feelings with anyone. We prayed together, and I gave my life back to my Lord, said I was sorry I had moved away from Him, and recommitted myself to follow Him with all my heart. I was determined to stay close to Him, and it would be visible. I was thirteen years old at the time.

In my faith, we are baptised fully in water to show our seriousness in wanting to follow Jesus and His ways. I wanted to do this.

Reflection:
1. Look up Psalm 51, where David repents after falling away from God, and God gives him a clean heart and right spirit. I needed this. What about you?
2. In three of four gospels (Injil) in the Bible, Jesus' baptism was recorded due to its significance. It shows how important it is. Take time to look into it.

Standing Up For Your Faith

Be on your guard; stand firm in the faith; be courageous; be strong. Do everything in love.
1 Corinthians 16:13–14

When I was growing up, my mother felt led by God to paint a Bible verse on a large rock by our post box at the edge of our drive and footpath, for all to see. Living in New Zealand, the letter box was at the end of the drive, and most people lived on a large plot of land, so we had a long driveway to get to the house.

I don't think the verse bothered me much, but in my early teens, it became an embarrassment, as kids threw rubbish at it.

She did it to remind people of Jesus. It was her way of showing her love for Jesus in her faith. She loved our home; it was hers, and she loved the Lord and wanted everyone to know she was a Jesus follower. The Bible verse she chose was to encourage people that no matter what they were going through, Jesus never changes: "Jesus Christ is the same yesterday and today and forever" (Hebrews 13:8). I don't know why she chose that verse, but I think it brought her a lot of comfort in an ever-changing world.

2. A letter to the church in Corinth by a follower of Jesus.

Sadly, once I started high school, which had just opened down the street from us, the violence against our home became worse. Students heaved their rubbish at our house. Threats hurled at me when I came home from school. The power of the words from the Bible annoyed people, and my mother had to paint over the words on the rock for our safety. It broke her heart to have to do this.

Reflection:

1. How can words about Jesus on a rock offend people?
2. Why was it so important to my mother to do this for all to see?
3. Do you think it was right for my mother to feel like she had to paint over these words?

He Is More Than A Ruler-Maker

But Jesus . . . said to the man with the shrivelled hand, "Get up and stand in front of everyone." So he got up and stood there. Then Jesus said to them, "I ask you, which is lawful on the Sabbath: to do good or to do evil, to save life or to destroy it?" He looked around at them all, and then said to the man, "Stretch out your hand." He did so, and his hand was completely restored.
Luke 6:8–10

When I was a child, we went to church every Sunday.
It made me think God was only happy with me when I went to church. It must be on His list of rules, and we had no choice but to go. It was incredibly dull, especially if there was no Sunday school for kids, and I had to sit through the whole service. He seemed to be a God who watched our every move, ready to show His disapproval at any moment. My upbringing was to do nothing on a Sunday. It was the Sabbath. Mum worked five days a week. She would frantically do all the housework on Saturdays, so there would be nothing left to do on Sunday. We weren't allowed to meet up with friends or watch TV. The whole neighbourhood was quiet; you could not hear a lawn mower. None of the shops were open on a Sunday. When they finally did open, my mother bought a Sunday paper, hid it in her bag till she came home, and then felt guilty the whole time she enjoyed reading it. If we went away over a weekend, she would find a church for us to attend.

It wasn't until I went to Australia to attend a Bible school, did my washing on a Sunday, and didn't go to church that I saw how God didn't strike me with lightning. Maybe I should get to know Him better, I thought.

God gave me a prayer I prayed daily: "Help me to know who You are. Break any false images of who I think You are, so that I might understand for myself, and tell others what You are like."

Reflection:

1. What do you think God is like?
2. In the Bible verses at the top of the story, Jesus heals someone on the Sabbath; what does that show us about God?
3. Could you pray the prayer I prayed to know what God is like?

The Not-So-Interested Becomes Willing

Then I heard the voice of the Lord saying, "Whom shall I send? And who will go for us?" And I said, "Here am I. Send me!"
Isaiah 6:8

It looked like it would be another boring church service. I looked around, but none of my friends were there. It was a warm summer evening in Napier, New Zealand, a city by the sea. As I settled in my seat, I heard seagulls squawking and remembered seeing them flying away from the church towards the beach—going where I wanted to go. I just needed to get through this service. It was the last Sunday before the Christmas school holidays in the southern hemisphere. All the studying was behind me, and then I could go to the beach like the seagulls whenever I wanted to. I was sixteen.

The preacher was good, but my mind drifted to warm summer days at the beach. Suddenly, I heard him say, "Finally . . ."

Thank God for the word finally. Usually, this meant his last sentence was coming, although I had been fooled by false hope before.

He said, "God was able to use Mary, Jesus' mother, because she was willing and available."

As soon as I heard those words, I heard myself saying, "I'm willing and available to You, God, to go and do whatever You ask me to do."

I hadn't come in feeling ready to do anything for God, but the words "willing and available" seemed a simple thing to offer God.

Reflection:
1. Can you trust God to care for you if you say you're willing and available?
2. If you have never done this, could this be what God is asking of you now?

I Need God to Change My Heart

Praise the Lord, my soul, and forget not all his benefits.
Psalm 103:2

Camping away from home was very different for us. We weren't like other families. Some people may have thought, She's lucky; she stays in a motel and doesn't have to camp in a tent.

But I longed to go camping, cook outside, sleep under the stars, and wake up to the birds singing.

Once, as a teenager, I was facing embarrassment that God had given me a father who wasn't like other fathers. My father was a quadriplegic. He was paralysed from the neck down, but he had some upper-body strength to enable him to drag his legs along. We needed ground floor places with wheelchair access and a roll-in shower. We always had a spare pair of trousers, as he refused to wear a catheter.

We didn't stop much along the way; the goal was to get where we were staying as quickly as possible. We did eat out a lot, so I was lucky, mainly because Mum had a habit of burning the dinner most nights. She loved to boil the food on high, read a book, and unfortunately forget about it. When Dad sat in his wheelchair, people often thought he had learning difficulties. They had no idea that he was a war hero, and there was nothing wrong with his brain. On one occasion, on holiday, we went

into a clothes shop to buy a suit for my brother's wedding. I was pushing the wheelchair, as it was a narrow shop.
The shopkeeper asked me, "How can I help him?"
I said, "Ask him."

Reflection:
1. Are there times when you think other families have it better than you do?
2. What can you do with this?
3. Why not stop and count your blessings?

Choosing A Job

In their hearts humans plan their course, but
the Lord establishes their steps.
Proverbs 16:9

It was a chance to buy a new dress. I was not interested in the advertised position; it would simply be a practice interview in my new dress. Mum drove me to the interview. We pulled up in front of an old wooden building with big glass windows. I could smell freshly cut wool from sheep, and cigarette smoke.

It was a distributor of wool bales: a small, family-owned company that needed a junior clerk. I had no idea what that meant; after all, it was only a practice interview. I don't remember listening to the interviewer and what the job entailed. Relaxed, I kept gazing down at the pretty new dress I had insisted my mother get for me. Before I knew it, he stood up, shook my hand, and said he'd be in touch.

To my horror and dismay, I got the job. I may have been the only one who had applied for it. Anyway, I soon found out what I would do every day: collect the mail, make coffee or tea for everyone in the office, type orders, and deliver invoices to businesses around town.

After six months, I was questioning my job choice. I was sitting at my desk typing when I said to God, "Lord, is this all I'm ever going to do?" I felt God impressed on my heart, "One day, a nurse."

Like Sarah in the Bible, when God told her "one day, a son" when she was too old to bear children, I laughed. My mother had been a nurse, and I'd only heard about the hard times she'd had. I didn't want that, but the idea grew and grew in my heart with excitement and peace. I went and did my nursing training.

Reflection:

1. Where was God in this story?
2. Did God lead me to the first job?
3. God loves to be in every part of our lives, including important decisions, like where shall I work? Compare the times you have invited Him into the decision and when you have not.

In My Dark Place

"I have set before you life and death . . . Choose life,
so that you and your children may live."
Deuteronomy 30:19b

Why did he go back to her? What was wrong with me?

I was so hurt, so low, and consumed with these questions. We met at a Christian youth gathering. We ended up sitting next to each other on the bus and talking. He had just broken up with someone. We were soon dating. I was so happy, but now it was over—just like that.

As we were saying goodbye after a lovely evening with friends, he told me he had decided to go back to his last girlfriend. I was in shock and devastated. I decided to end my life. It was too difficult. How could this be happening to me again? There had to be something wrong with me.

I sat in the dark in the car as thoughts of death filled my head. What's the point of living? I'm ugly. No one will even miss me. I don't fit in.

Then, I started to think about how I would do it. I could gas myself in the car or take Mum's sleeping pills. The pills sounded easier.

Darkness seemed to consume me, like I no longer had a choice to live. Repeatedly, words started to come into my head: just do it. JUST DO IT!

I went into the house to look for the pills. My mother was still awake and sensed things weren't okay. She listened as I told her how I was no longer with my boyfriend, but I didn't tell her how I wanted to die.

I fell asleep and woke up feeling numb. Prompted by God and a heaviness that would not leave me, I found a trusted friend to share what had happened.

She invited me to pray with her. She suggested I tell God I was sorry for my thoughts of death, tell Him I chose life and that I trust Him that He has a future planned out for me.

I did this, and the weight of death lifted off me. His love and presence seemed so close. I felt free to live again.

Reflection:

1. Have you ever felt this way?
2. Where was God in this?
3. Have you been—or are you still—in this place where life feels too complicated, and you want to end it? Get help. Tell someone and tell God. He wants to help, and He wants us to live.

Not My Time To Go Yet

The angel of the Lord encamps around those who fear him, and he delivers them.
Psalm 34:7

After I left college, I started my first job in my hometown in New Zealand. I was saving for my first car but still didn't have enough money, so I biked to and from work five days a week.

If you saw how I rode a bike and how many mishaps I've avoided, you would be right in thinking I have a very busy guardian angel!

I was 18 years old and was happily biking home from work. It was peak traffic at the end of the working day on one of two main roads through my city.

Suddenly, a car turned to go around the corner in front of me, when it was evident that I had the right of way. He drove straight into me. I flew over the bonnet, and my head hit the road, but it felt like it happened in slow motion. When my head hit the road, it seemed to land on an invisible cushion and slowly fell to the ground. It was as though someone had placed it there for me.

I knew it was real. Someone else was there with me. I got up, although this wouldn't have been possible without someone helping me from the ground. I think it was my guardian angel.

Reflection:

1. Have you ever experienced something like this?
2. Can you see God's hand protecting you over the years?
3. Count your blessings as you record His protection over your life.

Finding God For Myself

But if from there you seek the Lord your God, you will find him if you seek him with all your heart and with all your soul.
Deuteronomy 4:29

It was time to leave to start nursing, and I was full of emotions. I was scared and sad to leave my parents but excited to make my own decisions. What would leaving home be like? I had been brought up in a God-fearing home and attended a church that seemed to believe we were the only ones going to heaven, as we had the right message from God. Everyone else was wrong. We had nothing to do with anyone outside of our church.

My world was small and safe, and we liked it that way. The world was frightening and dangerous. Leaving home was huge for me as I entered this unknown, scary world.

After Mum and Dad left the nursing hostel where I would live, I went straight to my room and locked the door. The first evening was terrible. I didn't know anybody. We would start class in the morning. I imagined there could be initiations for new students and was terrified someone would put my head down the toilet.

I felt so out of my depth in the morning, living in this hostel. I thought God had made an awful mistake, and I wanted to go home. How would my faith work here? Where was God? Did He only live in godly places, like my home and places of worship?

I was okay when busy with classes, but when Saturday came, all the questions about God came back. Did this big, holy God in the sky care about me in this sinful place? Would this holy God dare communicate to me here? He seemed so far away from me.

I was lonely. My classmates wanted to go to the pub and drink, and I hadn't done anything like that before. I stayed in my room. I read my Bible and my daily readings. Maybe God would meet me here.

He did. The words from the Bible spoke to me, and I felt I needed to press into Him more. He was here, in this place. I would need to find Him beyond what a human preached each Sunday, or my parents taught me. I needed my faith to move the longest distance in the world—from my head to my heart.

Reflection:

1. How do you find God beyond your family's beliefs and traditions?
2. Have you ever prayed for God to reveal Himself to you?

If He Wants You There, Nothing Will Stop It

Jesus looked at them and said, "With man this is impossible, but with God all things are possible."
Matthew 19:26

"How do I make a choice? This organisation is all over the world. Where am I meant to go?"
It would be my first time being away from New Zealand.
Australia was the closest; plus, my brother lived there with his wife if I needed help. There were three bases of the organisation there. "I'll apply to all three."
The base in Brisbane (where my brother lived) accepted me after receiving a complete application. The other two bases never received all the applications. One got lost in the mail.
It was obvious where I was to go.
I had applied for a British passport because my dad came from England. It seemed fun. I sounded like a world traveller with two passports. I might only ever go back to NZ and never travel the world, but you never know, I thought.

But now the problem was this: I used my British passport to apply for my application to Australia, so now I needed a visa to go there. If I had used my NZ passport, I wouldn't have needed a visa for Australia.

I now had a week before I was to leave, and my passport with the visa to Australia wasn't back yet. I phoned the visa office to discover processing would typically take six weeks. I panicked, cried, and then prayed, in that order. All the doubts came flying into my mind. I'm not going, am I? What do I tell people? I resigned from my nursing job; what will I do now? Maybe I don't know how to follow God.

I got everyone I knew who could breathe to pray. Getting the visa before I was to leave would be a miracle.

Two days later, the passport arrived with a visa for Australia—the day before I was to go. A miracle had happened.

Reflection:

1. What can you learn from this?
2. What happened that changed everything?
3. How can you apply this to your situation: now, or in the future?

Your Inheritance Is Part of His Plan

Lord, you alone are my portion and my cup; you make my lot secure. The boundary lines have fallen for me in pleasant places; surely I have a delightful inheritance.
Psalm 16:5–6

My grandmother was a housemaid in a wealthy manor in Ireland, and my grandfather, the family's oldest son, owned the manor. They were not allowed to interact much at all together.

They fell in love. One night, they ran away together to get married and boarded a ship to New Zealand. Due to this action, my grandfather was disinherited from his family's wealth. With no farming skills, they settled in a small country town called Levin and soon had eight children, my mother being the second youngest.

Grandmother already had six kids by the time my mother was to come into this world; she wasn't wanted, but God wanted her to be born. God planned for her to bring two more generations into this world, too—me and my son—both miracle children.

The faith my family chose to follow resulted from St. Patrick coming to Ireland to tell the Irish about Christianity in the 400s AD. It wasn't until my grandmother moved to NZ that she became a faithful Jesus follower, after a couple from a local church came to visit her home. My mother was nine years old then; she was doing the dishes and overhearing the conversation about Jesus, and she decided to become a Jesus follower, too.

Reflection:

1. Do you know your family's story?
2. Can you see how God has been part of your inheritance?
3. Can you accept the family you came from—the good and bad parts?

Just What I Needed to Hear

If I rise on the wings of the dawn, if I settle on the far side of the sea,
even there your hand will guide me, your right hand will hold me fast.
Psalm 139:9–10

I was leaving New Zealand for the first time to live overseas. My upbringing meant I had been relatively sheltered from the world. We belonged to a select church group and did not mix with anyone outside. I had moved away to do nursing, but it was only an hour-and-a-half car journey, so I could get home quickly. I also thought the second time I would leave home would be to marry, but instead, I followed what I sensed was from God: heading to Australia to attend a Bible college to learn more about my Christian faith.

I did not know how to connect with God yet, but I always followed a daily Bible reading. As I sat on the plane, shaken up from leaving, I turned to the lesson for the day.

I read Matthew 28:5: "The angel said to the women, 'Do not be afraid, for I know that you are looking for Jesus, who was crucified.'" These words brought immediate reassurance that I was on the right path. God was reminding me we are in this together.

I had no idea what I was getting myself into, but knowing He was with me was all I needed to hear.

Reflection:

1. What do we learn about God in this story?
2. Why would this make a difference?
3. How can I apply this to my life today?
4. Do these verses from the Bible bring you comfort?

He's Not Just Sitting in Heaven

IfThe Lord is near to all who call on him, to all who call on him in truth. He fulfils the desires of those who fear Him; he hears their cry and saves them.
Psalm 145:18–19

My earliest memory of talking to God is when I was six. I asked Him to be the boss of my life. Because I was rather bossy with others, this was probably the right move. I knew He was BIG and lived in heaven, which was a long way away from me. And I knew that He probably had no interest in my everyday life. Growing up, I interpreted from my church and mother that we had our ticket to heaven, so we just needed to grin and bear what came our way till we went to heaven.

One day, when I was 20 years old, I heard an outstanding teaching: God wanted to be a part of our everyday life here. He had created me to have a relationship with Him, as when He walked with Adam and Eve in the Garden of Eden.

I left the room and realised I wanted this relationship with God more than anything. "I don't know how to get closer to You, so please teach me," I prayed. I didn't realise I was praying for Him to teach me how to trust Him and see Him as the only answer for what I needed.

I was living simply as a volunteer so I could give my time to serving in the Bible college, and I was running out of money. I needed toothpaste—a basic necessity in life—and had no idea where I would get the money to buy it. When I came back from lunch break to my room, there on my pillow was money to buy toothpaste, a stamp for a letter home, and a bit left over.

This miracle would be the first of many miracles of provision that I would see God perform.

Reflection:

1. What can you learn about God in this story?
2. What was the transformation I saw in my own heart that changed everything?
3. What do you get out of the Bible verses in Psalm 145 at the top of the page?
4. How can you apply this view of God in your life?

One Lettuce, One Carrot, and Five Tomatoes

Taking the five loaves and the two fish and looking up to heaven, he gave thanks and broke the loaves. Then he gave them to his disciples to distribute to the people. He also divided the two fish among them all. They all ate and were satisfied.
Mark 6:41–42

It was my turn to do weekend duties at the Bible school in Brisbane, Australia. I went to the kitchen. The head cook said I had one lettuce, one carrot, and five tomatoes to make a salad for 30 people. My mother loved the salad and could have eaten half of that for her dinner on her own. How would this feed 30 people?

We cut it up and put it into a large bowl, which looked rather silly, and prayed over it that it would feed us all. I didn't have a lot of faith that it would, but I put it on the table for lunch.

When we were about to eat, a team of 12 joined us. It was already doubtful that this food could feed 30 people, much less 42 people. We prayed, gave thanks to God, and started to serve lunch.

As each person dipped into the bowl, I thought it would soon be gone, but the salad bowl did not empty. Not just a few leaves, either. I couldn't believe my eyes. The bowl was as full as it had been when we served it. I was utterly amazed. God did it again, just like in the Bible. He fed the multitude, and there were leftovers.

Reflection:
1. When there is no other choice but for God to move, how does that make you feel?
2. God can still move with the weakest of faith. Has that happened to you? Recall the story to yourself.
3. When did you last trust God to move in your life when there were no other choices? Did He come through?

Snakes Will Not Harm You

They will pick up snakes with their hands; and when they drink deadly poison, it will not hurt them at all.
Mark 16:18a [3]

Our school in Brisbane, Australia, was heading out to go and share our faith in the neighbourhood. I wanted to do it well so people would be open to hearing more about the good news of Jesus coming to earth.
In the Bible, Jesus sent out His followers two by two, so we decided to do the same. To be safe, we paired up a girl with a boy, and the two groups were always close to each other.
Aaron and I were feeling quite nervous as we approached our first home when a snake reared up and hissed at us as we went to knock at the door. Petrified, I jumped back as my friend jumped in the way of the snake. The snake tried to attack us both, but with some loud prayers and lots of noise, it retreated. We retreated as well, too shaken to speak to the people inside.
After thanking God for protecting us and taking a moment to compose ourselves, we moved on to the next house. Once all the teams were back at the Bible college, we shared our story and concluded that the folks inside this house needed God, so we prayed for them and planned to return to them another time.

3 Jesus was speaking to his disciples of His protection over them as they went out to share their faith just before He ascended to heaven.

Reflection:

1. Can you see how God can protect you when you step out for Him?
2. There can often be repercussions when we step out for God, but always remember that God is more powerful than anything else.

Just Set the Table

Then the word of the Lord came to Elijah: "Leave here, turn eastward and hide in the Kerith Ravine, east of the Jordan. You will drink from the brook, and I have directed the ravens to supply you with food there." So he did what the Lord had told him. He went to the Kerith Ravine, east of the Jordan, and stayed there. The ravens brought him bread and meat in the morning and bread and meat in the evening, and he drank from the brook.
1 Kings 17:2–6

The dinner bell rang, and we usually went straight to the dining room, but this time, we were to go into the lounge to pray. Our leader told us we had two Australian dollars left in the bank account, so we needed to see a miracle to feed us all that night. There were about 50 of us in our 20s and 30s, plus children in this Bible School in Brisbane.

We prayed, rejoiced, and went and set the table for dinner. We all found a place at the table and thanked God for His provision. I don't know that I fully comprehended the faith of these people. I just knew I was hungry. We waited, talked, and enjoyed each other for about an hour. Suddenly, a loud knock at the door startled us into silence. Someone went to the door. A lady was standing there with a box of pumpkins. Everyone screamed with joy, and the box disappeared towards the kitchen. The cooks got to work. They made pumpkin soup and pumpkin bread. God had come through. He had heard our prayers and rewarded our faith.

God loves us believing in Him to come through. Sometimes, all it takes is an act of faith and setting the table.

Reflection:

1. How would you feel if you were in this story—at the beginning, middle, and end?
2. Would it change your opinion of God as your provider? If so, what would that mean to you right now in your situation?
3. Why is having faith in God and His ways so important to Him?

God Cares About Our Comfort

The Lord is my shepherd, I lack nothing. He makes me lie down in green pastures, he leads me beside quiet waters, he refreshes my soul.
Psalm 23:1–3a

I travelled 52 hours from my Bible school in Brisbane by bus to visit my auntie and uncle in Adelaide, and it was tough for my back. When I was a nurse, I had slipped a disc, and sitting for long periods was now challenging for me.

Auntie and my uncle gave me such a wonderful week, and on Sunday, they took me to their church. One of the leaders asked me to share a story from my time in Brisbane at the Bible school. I was thrilled to have the opportunity, as it might persuade someone else to go and do the same.

The following day, I was to travel the gruelling journey back to Brisbane. That night, I dreamed I was on an aeroplane and arrived home, rested and refreshed.

When I woke, my aunt told me there was an envelope for me in their letterbox. There was a note thanking me for sharing in church, and it contained enough money for a flight back to Brisbane.

God had granted me a comfortable trip home instead of a long bus ride, from an anonymous giver.

Reflection:

1. Where do you see God in this story?
2. What did the dream have to do with the story?
3. What God orchestrated here: how would it make you feel?

I Can Do More Than This

Whoever can be trusted with very little can also be trusted with much.
Luke 16:10a

Do you ever feel like you were made for more than this? I was 20 years old and raring to go into something BIG for God. I was not married, did not have kids, and was healthy and fit. Bring it on, God! I am ready for whatever You have for me to do. I will be Your hands and feet here on earth.

During weekly announcements in the dining room, someone said, "We need someone to assist our preschool teacher four times a week while the parent students are in lectures."

I stood up and said, "I will do it!" I was expecting the staff to burst into applause, but at the same time, I was thinking that God would soon find me something more suitable for my giftings.

I had yet to learn the position was for three months. I was a glorified babysitter. That's all I was. I changed nappies, played with the kids, took them for walks, and drew pictures with them. Surely God had something more important for me to do?

One evening, I was walking down the stairs to the hall for dinner when a poster came off the wall and landed at my feet. The verse was from a letter from a follower of Jesus to a church he led in Galatia: "Let us not become weary in doing good, for at the proper time we will reap a harvest if we do not give up" (Galatians 6:9).

Okay, God, loud and clear: I need to stay doing what I am doing with all my heart, until You say otherwise.

Reflection:

1. Do you ever think God is too slow at getting you to the place where you will excel?
2. Do you wonder why He's not using you more for Him?
3. Name some things God may want to teach you, using the time you're in now.
4. What was God trying to say through the Bible verse, and how does this relate to my story?

Creating and Being Creative

God saw all that he had made, and it was very good.
Genesis 1:31a

He has filled them with skill to do all kinds of work
as engravers, designers, embroiderers . . .
Exodus 35:35

I was a lonely kid, as my siblings were a lot older than me. So, from a young age, I would sit on our swing in the back garden and make up songs. I would go into my world and simply sing out what was happening inside me. It made me feel better.

When I was 20 years old, I wrote a song that I needed to sing to people as a testimony of what God had done in my life. I called the song "Princess." It painted a story of a girl invited by the King (God) to come and do things with Him. This was something she did not feel worthy of or capable of doing.

In the song, I said that He doesn't leave me to work it out alone. He gives me clothes (encouragement/praise) and equipment (Bible verses) to do it with, so I have all I need to work together with Him.

I love the movie Chariots of Fire, especially when Eric Liddell's sister reprimands him by telling him he's neglecting his responsibilities before God as he devotes his focus to competitive running. Liddell responds,

"I believe that God made me for a purpose. But He also made me fast, and when I run, I feel His pleasure."

Reflection:
1. Did you ever think about how much fun God must have had creating the world? I wonder if He smiled as He created a stick insect or an anteater. What were they made for? Maybe it was just His creative licence, making them to please Him.
2. What if what we did was simply for fun? Do you think God would see it as a waste of time? What if we used our talents simply to please Him?

A Change of Heart

I will give you a new heart and put a new spirit in you; I will remove from you your heart of stone and give you a heart of flesh.
Ezekiel 36:26

At the Bible school in Brisbane, Australia, a year earlier, it was my turn to clean the toilets. I remember scrubbing the men's bathroom floor on my knees, retching as I did it. I wanted to kick the toilet and yell at God: I didn't come here to do this!

I wanted to be seen as a great person in the eyes of my church, doing mighty things for God so I would have exhilarating stories to tell. Not this.

When I heard the need for a nurse in the Philippines I said, "Here I am. Send me!" (The prophet Isaiah says this to the Lord in Isaiah 6:8.) Joyfully, I got all my vaccinations. I had no idea where the Philippines was or what I would do there. I even wrote a newsletter where I misspelt the word and called it "Philippians"; friends thought I was going to Greece! Here I was again. It was my turn to clean the toilets, and a dread overcame me. It was so hot, with the humidity and temperatures in the 40s, that I had to scrub at 7.30 am. It was even worse here than in Australia, as used toilet paper went into a bucket beside the toilet so it didn't block the toilet. I had to empty these buckets, then clean around the toilet bowl that didn't work that well after a flush.

But this time, it was different. God had changed my heart, and I sang as I cleaned.

Whatever You want me to do, Lord, I'll do it. Whatever You want me to say, Lord, I'll say it. Wherever You want me to go, Lord, I'll go.

Reflection:

1. What changed my heart?

2. No matter how much effort we put into trying to be a better person having the right attitude, why isn't this enough to change us?

A Still, Small Voice

Whether you turn to the right or to the left, your ears will hear a voice behind you, saying, "This is the way; walk in it."
Isaiah 30:21

The mother shrieked, "Help me, help me!"

There was no other medical staff in Manila, Philippines, at the community development centre when she came in. It was up to me. My nursing skills were limited. I didn't have tropical medicine nursing training.

A lady with a seven-month-old baby—but weighing the amount of a seven-week-old baby—had come to the door. The baby was severely malnourished, had a fever, was breathing frantically, and was pathetically trying to get out a cry.

"Lord, what do I do?"

An authoritative, calm voice spoke in my ear. It was my Lord telling me step by step what to do. "You need to get his temperature down. Give him a tepid bath." Next, God led me to get an eye dropper and give small amounts of water into his mouth.

Step by step, I did as He told me. The baby began to respond and calm down. He fell asleep in my arms but was still struggling with his breathing. I still needed to take him to the hospital. God had got me through the crisis part with this child, and I got him to the hospital for further treatment.

Reflection:

1. Where was God in the crisis?
2. How does the Bible verse relate to this story?
3. Remember when God was there when you needed Him? Trust He will lead you step by step when you need Him again.

He Gives Us Words in Difficult Times

Blessed are those who mourn, for they will be comforted.
Matthew 5:4

One evening, while working in the Philippines, one of the staff asked a few of us to go to a house where they had just lost their son to a stabbing in a robbery incident. The family needed someone to take a church service for them. I remember travelling across Manila by Jeepney and feeling very insecure about what we would say.
The family were so pleased that we had come. They were a wealthier family than I was used to and welcomed us into their lovely home.
In the middle of the lounge lay their son in an open coffin.
We quietly sang some familiar songs, and then I felt led to read Psalm 23 and share some words of comfort from this passage. It was the first time I had done anything like this before. I listened to myself as the words came out, but I was conscious these words were very much from God. After such an awful loss, what could anyone say? Only God knew the best thing to say to bring them some form of comfort. After we concluded the service with prayer, we listened to them as they told us about him, then wept and ate together.

Reflection:
1. God may have given us a great mind and eloquent words, but without Him behind them, they are just a noise. Have you noticed this difference when trying to help someone?
2. Can you take comfort in this verse?

4 Jesus said these words.

5 A small bus made by converting an army Jeep left by the Americans.

His Word Is Alive and Active

Every word of God is flawless; he is a shield
to those who take refuge in him.
Proverbs 30:5

Your word is a lamp for my feet, a light on my path.
Psalm 119:105

I've never been one to memorise Bible verses, but I think it a good idea to have a few up your sleeve to call on. One such incident was when I was living in Manila. I was travelling around town, and our motto was: Most of the time, pray and keep your eyes low.

I noticed a handsome man, and soon, I focused my mind on his form. The thoughts were so strong, and I knew they were wrong. I didn't know what to do, but then I remembered someone saying to think on God's Word, and the thoughts would flee. The verse that came to mind was, "Let us fix our eyes on Jesus, the author and perfecter of our faith" (Hebrews 12:2, BSB). I repeated it several times, and my mind became free.

I don't think what you quote matters, even if it's "The Lord is my Shepherd." His words are so powerful, and this is proof that it works—quickly, and when you need it.

6 Hebrews is a book in the Bible written to encourage Jewish believers. Its author is unknown but is thought to be Paul, a church leader.

Reflection:

1. Joyce Meyer, a well-known author and speaker, discusses our "Stinkin' Thinkin'" and wrote a book called The Battle of the Mind. I believe we all struggle with our thoughts, but this story gives you hope that God's Word from the Bible can protect your mind.
2. In several religions, you can find the value of memorisation. Let's keep some of the Bible in our hearts and minds.

God Is More Powerful than Any Evil Spirits

You are my hiding place; you will protect me from trouble and surround me with songs of deliverance.
Psalm 32:7

When I was 21 years old, working in a free clinic for the poor in the Philippines, I had an experience that confirmed that God can overcome any evil spirit.

An American woman not much older than I had just arrived to help in the clinic to serve as a pharmacist. We soon got to know each other. She had recently divorced her husband, but every night, she kept having nightmares. I felt led by God to ask her a bit about her husband. He had been in the occult for a while. I felt from God that I needed to pray with her to break off soul ties from the union they had together in their marriage.

Again, not knowing what to do but feeling confident in the Lord, I suggested she ask the Lord to forgive her for getting involved with a man who was into things that were not godly and cut off the soul ties [7] she had with him in the heavenly realm. She did this.

The next day, she sought me out to tell me she had slept deeply without any nightmares.

When we are fully committed to following God and His ways, we don't have to put up with the presence of any evil spirits. "The one who is in you is greater than the one who is in the world" (1 John 4:4). [8]

[7] When we have sex with someone, we become one; we join not only our bodies together but our spirits, too, referred to as "soul ties."

[8] A disciple of Jesus writes this in a letter to the saints in the Bible.

Reflection:

1. In Genesis (the first book of the Bible/Torah) and Mark's gospel, Jesus speaks of becoming one flesh: "That is why a man leaves his father and mother and is united to his wife, and they become one flesh" (Genesis 2:24). This story demonstrates this. What can we do to ensure we won't be affected in this way by another spirit?
2. How do we guard ourselves from any ungodly spirits? This includes seeking other ways of discovering the future: reading horoscopes, tea leaves, palms, or going to a fortune teller or psychic.

A Welcomed Storm

The Lord will guide you always; he will satis-
fy your needs in a sun-scorched land
and will strengthen your frame. You will
be like a well-watered garden,
like a spring whose waters never fail.
Isaiah 58:11

Before they call, I will answer; while they are speaking I will hear.
Isaiah 65:24

Every day from February to April 1985 in the Philippines, I worked in a free medical clinic with a Filipino doctor to help sick babies and small children. I worked long afternoons from 2 pm until 7 pm, with over 50 families coming daily. It was also scorching, the hottest I had ever experienced.

Monsoon season was approaching; the weather began to change, and droves of mosquitoes came with it. Early morning and evening were the worst times. At one point, a mosquito carrying dengue fever bit me. I woke in the middle of the night with a fever and was quite delirious. I could see what looked like monsters on the walls and thought I heard mean laughter coming from them. I had a fever of 103 degrees and aches all over. I couldn't eat. Everything tasted bitter. I lay on my bed and slept on and off for a week. I prayed, God, please send rain and cool the air.

God heard my prayer when I had barely spoken it out loud. The torrential rain came, the mosquitoes left, and the temperature dropped. It was a welcome relief. Ten days later, I almost returned to myself with no lingering symptoms from dengue fever.

Reflection:

1. Does God have authority over the weather?
2. In Mark's gospel, chapter 4, Jesus calms the storm when the disciples think they will drown. But His presence can calm any storm in our lives, not just the weather. If you feel like you are in a "storm," call on God to help you through it.
3. Remember how He has helped you and wants to do it again when you call on Him.

Learning More About Prayer

Look to the Lord and his strength; seek his face always.
1 Chronicles 16:11 [9]

Seeking God about the future through prayer was still a new concept. I was more of a "move forward first" kind of girl, reasoning that if God is not in it, He'll close the door.

A confident, yet gentle, American lady came to the staff while I worked in the Philippines. She came to simply pray for the community we were working in, and for staff who wanted prayer, as they were helping the poor through the free medical clinic and giving out food and clothing. I decided I wanted to grow in this area of prayer, so I asked her to pray with me. My question to the Lord was, "What do you have next for me?" Without us saying a word to each other, England soon came to her mind and then to mine. I even felt like weeping for the country. I had never done this before, and my prayer for this nation was deep and passionate.

I also saw a picture of an old brick building in my mind and knew it had something to do with my future. The lady also felt that I would go there. As she said these words, a feeling of joy came to my soul.

Not long after this, one of the staff based in Manila, where I was, returned from England with a booklet on a Bible school in the Midlands. I looked through it and was struck by how good the school sounded. I had realised how much I needed to know the Bible more.

I applied and was accepted. Step by step, the Lord led me in ways I could have never foreseen.

The building I pictured in my mind during prayer was the one I would work and live in after I had finished the Bible school, confirming I was still in His will.

But that's another story.

[9] This was written by the prophet Ezra.

Reflection:

1. Do you think God wants to tell you about your future? He does, and He wants us to be confident and not left guessing.
2. Invite Him into your decision-making.

Change of Direction

But Naomi said, "Return home, my daughters."
Ruth 1:11a [10]

In the Philippines, I worked most days in a clinic with a doctor giving free care to the locals and most evenings in the red-light district, sharing my faith with the street workers. I was in my element and very content. Then I got the dreaded "dengue fever," which is in an earlier story. I came up with this brilliant idea: to be able to stay, I could move to the mountain area of the Philippines, where there were very few mosquitos, and I could help a lady working alone there.

But God had another idea.

In my daily reading that day, I was reading from the book of Ruth when suddenly the words in bold letters leapt out of the page: "Go home, daughter."

"God, wouldn't I be more use to You here? Shouldn't I stay till they find a nurse who will replace me?" I asked.

I was learning to recognise when there is peace and joy, with complete understanding, it is probably God's leading.

My mother had organised a return flight, which I would have ignored, but now it looked like I needed it.

Then, as we were about to drive to the airport, a woman stepped into the house and said, "I'm a nurse. Can I help?"

God also made sure the clinic wasn't without a nurse.

Reflection:

1. Can you see how keeping a regular Bible reading can help you see God's leading?
2. Be ready and open to God changing your plans at any moment. His ways are always best.

[10] Ruth is in Jesus's genealogy.

Was She an Angel?

For he will command his angels concerning you to guard you in all your ways.
Psalm 91:11

It was my first long-haul flight. I was 21 years old and heading to England from NZ via the USA. I had a cheap flight, which equates to a lengthy journey. I had a stopover in Hawaii. I knew the headquarters of the Bible school I was to attend in England was in Hawaii, but I had no idea where, nor that there was more than one island in Hawaii. When God said Go, I never bothered to educate myself about the journey; I just went.

I was so tired from the flight, the time difference, and the emotional goodbyes to friends and family. So much of the unknown was before me; I felt lonely. I needed to feel God's presence with me and find others doing what I was doing from the same organisation. Plus, I was desperate for somewhere to lay my head, so I decided to see if I could find the headquarters.

I found a telephone book (before mobile phones), got an address, and headed to the deserted bus stop outside the airport terminal with no idea what to do next. Suddenly, an older lady stood beside me. She said, "You're looking for the Bible school, aren't you?"

I was stunned and said yes. She said, "Follow me." Without hesitation, I followed her. She handed me money for the bus, something to eat, and said, "Get on this bus." I did; she got on with me. It seemed like a long ride, and I had no idea where I was going or how to get back to the airport.

Before she left, she told me to get off at the next stop. I looked out the window to see where it was and turned to say thank you. Just as quickly as she had appeared, she was gone. I wondered if she was an angel in human form. I stepped off the bus, and right in front of me stood the Bible school, as she had said.

They invited me in to eat, fellowship with them, sleep, and shower; then they drove me back to the airport that evening.

Reflection:

1. In this story, can you see how God is looking after me in practical ways?

2. Do you think if God calls you to leave home, He will care for you? He may even use an angel to do this.

Healing Through the Bible

Blessed is the one . . . whose delight is in the law of the Lord, and who meditates on his law day and night. That person is like a tree planted by streams of water, which yields its fruit in season and whose leaf does not wither— whatever they do prospers.
Psalm 1:1–3

I can sound very convincing because I learned to guess and bluff through school and jobs. I carried a heavy shame on my shoulders: I struggled to read.

I was now 22 years old. What I didn't know before I signed up for this Bible course was that I would have to read all 66 books in the Bible five times each, and the first time aloud.

People were going to find out about my secret. I felt so sick at the idea of us reading the Holy Scriptures out loud in groups. What if I couldn't say the words? Would they laugh at me like the others did in high school? I didn't know how I would bear it.

The group staff member leading could see me shaking before we even started. She graciously said to everyone, "If you can't say the word, just say wheelbarrow." I don't know how, but that kindness made me relax. I was soon using the word "wheelbarrow" quite a lot, and students started joining in. I think they probably knew the words I struggled with, but they wanted me to feel part of the group. It was so healing to my soul.

The Bible also brought healing in other ways. Reading it day by day meant you couldn't hide from what God wanted to point out in your life. I couldn't escape dealing with things, forgiving people, receiving His comfort for my pain and a deeper understanding of His love for the whole world.

Reflection:

1. If you have never tried reading the Bible, I recommend you do, especially the parts that you are allowed to in your faith: the Torah (the first five books of the Bible), the Prophets (major and minor), the Psalms, and the Injil ("gospels," the writings about Isa, or Jesus).

2. To Jesus's followers, the Bible is the living Word. It is inspired by God so that those who read it receive life out of it. Only with the help of God can we fully understand it, so it is good to pray while you are reading. Many of Jesus's followers try to remember parts of the Bible to recall to memory when it is needed. I give an example of this in another story in this book, when I worked in the Philippines.

What Is Clean Is Clean

Do not judge, or you too will be judged. For in the same way you judge others, you will be judged, and with the measure you use, it will be judged to you. Why do you look at the speck of sawdust in your brother's eye and pay no attention to the plank in your eye?
Matthew 7:1–3 [11]

I was dating someone, and we were happy together. As time passed, we shared more and more things from our lives.
I struggled as I heard about John's past life. I went away to talk to the Lord about it. I happened to be studying the book of Acts in the Bible at that time. I felt led to read Peter's vision in Acts [12] 10. The words in my head from verse 15 spoke loudly to my heart: "Do not call anything impure that God has made clean."
Who was I to be the judge? How could I hold his past against him? If God had made him clean, who was I to make him unclean again in my mind and heart?
Peter initially didn't understand what God meant by this vision or the words. He thought the good news of Jesus was only for the Jews, but God wanted to show him it was also for the Gentiles, for everyone.
No matter what we have done or what others have done to us, God can make any of us clean again.
In the Bible, in the book of Acts chapter 10 verses 34–35, we read: "I now realise how true it is that God does not show favouritism but accepts from every nation the one who fears him and does what is right."

Reflection:
1. What do you learn about yourself in this story?
2. What can we learn about God?

11 Jesus said these words.

12 Acts records the beginning of our church history in the Bible, written by Luke, a doctor who also wrote the gospel of Luke to a Roman official. Luke was a Jesus follower.

A Helpful Distraction

Be strong and courageous. Do not be afraid or terrified because of them, for the Lord your God goes with you; he will never leave you nor forsake you.
Deuteronomy 31:6

He has blinded their eyes and hardened their hearts, so they can neither see with their eyes nor understand with their hearts.
John 12:40a

I remember how nervous we were; our hearts were racing, our bodies trembling as we tried to look as calm as possible. We were travelling along the former Yugoslavian border when a guard from the Albanian side approached our car. Would he make us open the boot? God, please close his eyes to what is in there.

It was 1986. My boyfriend then had been learning Albanian for when the Iron Curtain of communism came down. We had been praying for this closed country when an opportunity came up to join an Italian woman and her team and go there. We planned to take a tourist bus through the country, pray, and leave tracts about our faith wherever possible. The only way into the country was on a four-day visa.

We had to make alternative plans as the team leader had her visa revoked. We would go along the border of Albania and pray God would lead us to people He wanted us to talk to. Enver Hoxha (the former Prime Minister of Albania) had declared that God was dead in his country; their religion was now Atheism. He closed the country to the West and its influences in 1967.

We did not believe this was right. Everyone needed the freedom of religion. We must do what we could to bring the truth to this nation. We would give out Bibles wherever we could. It was the Bibles that we had in the boot of the car that day.

Several guards had decided to check our passports and look over the car. We were travelling so much that I hadn't been able to dry my underwear, so I placed them on the back shelf of the car to dry as we drove. The guards became so distracted by my underwear that they never opened the boot.

We reversed out of there as quickly as we could, chuckling to ourselves at how my underwear had kept us safe from our real reason for being there.

Reflection:

1. In what ways have you seen God protect you? Take a moment to stop and reflect.

Laying Down Her Life

Do nothing out of selfish ambition or vain conceit. Rather, in humility value others above yourselves, not looking to your own interests but each of you to the interests of the others.
Philippians 2:3–4 [13]

Learn to do right; seek justice. Defend the oppressed. Take up the cause of the fatherless; plead the case of the widow.
Isaiah 1:17

We hadn't heard from Loretta for at least six weeks. We had spent the previous month together every day, so now it was odd to have this time of silence.

Loretta was a short, round Italian lady with greying hair, in her 30s but looking much older. Her skin was leathery from the harsh European sun, yet her eyes sparkled with a strong faith in God. Loretta had a massive heart for the Albanian people, who had not been allowed to hear about Jesus due to the communist rule of Enver Hoxha, the dictator who had closed Albania off to the rest of the world. Her mission was to get Christian Albanians out of Albania in whatever way she could.

Finally, a letter arrived from her telling us what happened. After we had said our goodbyes at the station, before she was able to get on to the train to head home, she was arrested, put into a Yugoslavian jail, and fed bread and water for a month—all because we were handing out Bibles to Albanians along the Yugoslavian side of the Albanian border. This was illegal and seen as spreading propaganda against communism. One line in this letter stands out the most to me: "I don't mind that I went through this, as it helped me understand what the people I'm trying to help go through all the time."

13 A letter to the church at Philippi from a church leader.

She had invited us to join her weeks before, but we had felt led by the Lord to decline the offer and return to England. God knew our lives were heading in other directions.

Reflection:

1. When you are trying to help in any situation, do you agree that having gone through that situation yourself can help the other person?
2. If our lives belong to God, and He wants to use us to help others, do you think there are some things we are to go through, good or bad, so we can have authority to speak in that area?

Warning Bells

When they had gone, an angel of the Lord appeared to Joseph in a dream. "Get up," he said, "take the child and his mother and escape to Egypt."
Matthew 2:13a

My heart was broken. I thought I would marry John. I so wanted to marry him. He was perfect: a real gentleman, everything I could have wanted. I knew he loved me, so why couldn't we be together? I knew the answer, but my head still wanted a good explanation.

There had been "warning bells," but I didn't want to listen. I had gone to see my uncle in Manchester, England, and John sent me a letter while I was there. He asked me to date him once I returned to Bible college. I was thrilled.

That night, I had a dream. In the dream, I saw us walking around the Bible college, and everyone was smiling and saying, "Don't they make a happy couple?"

Suddenly, I heard a voice say, "I am not in this."

I knew it was God. I woke in a sweat, saying, "No, no, no, it will be alright."

We pursued our friendship, and I was blissfully happy. I would make this work. John loved me, so I didn't need God's approval. He was a good man, and I was sure it would work out fine, and God would change His mind.

John had been studying the Albanian language while Albania was still closed to the West, ready for when it would open. He was an Oxford graduate and way out of my league. For some unknown reason, he enjoyed my company. We had heard of an outreach team going to Albania via Italy, and he wanted to go. I didn't have the money; in the past, this always confirmed whether God was in it. Another "warning bell."

Regardless, I would make it happen. I asked my parents for money, but it never arrived on time. I did not feel at peace about going on this outreach, but I was determined to go anyway.

While we were in Italy, he lost his peace about moving on in our relationship to marriage, and he asked for time apart to seek God for our future. Reluctantly, I agreed because I was scared things were about to change. In a dream, he saw a picture of us swimming out to sea, and God was on the shore. He came away from the dream with the sense from God that He wasn't in this. I was devastated. God had another plan for each of us, but not together.

God showed me in a dream that I was to return to England. He even showed me the same picture He'd given me in the Philippines two years earlier of the next house I would live in. Even in my disobedience (that God knew I would embrace), God had shown me the next step so I would see God was still very much with me. Genesis 3 in the Bible tells the story of Adam and Eve; when they sinned in the garden, God still made their clothes. Don't you just love that about God? He's so kind and merciful!

I got a job as a nurse to pay my way back home to NZ and lived in the building in England that God had shown me two years earlier in the Philippines. John moved to Albania when it opened and helped translate the Bible into the Albanian language.

Reflection:

1. What do we learn from how deliberately disobeying God can affect us?
2. Looking back, has God ever given you "warning bells" so you could avoid subsequent pain? Let God forgive you and comfort you for that mistake.
3. What do we learn about God working with His children when they disobey Him?

Close to the Broken-Hearted

The Lord is close to the broken-hearted and
saves those who are crushed in spirit.
Psalm 34:18

I became determined to get home to New Zealand by myself. It had been five months since we had separated, and my heart was still so raw, as though it had been yesterday.

Saving for the flight ticket home was a slower process than I expected, so I found a local church to attend. The service went along okay, but nothing settled in my heart. I kept questioning God why the relationship ended and whether I would ever find someone like him again.

Filled with pain and having no idea how I'd get over this, I went to the restroom and cried.

I can't explain what happened next, but it felt so real. Alone in the bathroom, I thought I was alone when God's love surrounded me as if the four walls were closing in on me to give me a huge hug. I tried to resist it, as I felt unworthy of His love. I had known God was never in our relationship from the beginning. Why would He care enough to comfort me, who had disobeyed Him and caused the pain I now found myself in? What kind of God is this?

I thought again of God reaching out to Adam and Eve after they sinned and made them clothes. He didn't have to. His love for us is so great. I fail Him over and over again. He keeps on loving me and reaching out to me. I eventually melted in His love and comfort with a grateful heart.

Reflection:

1. What can you learn about God from this?
2. Can you believe He will reach out to you like this when you need it?

He Did This for Me!

For what I received I passed on to you as of first importance: that Christ died for our sins according to the Scriptures, that he was buried, that he was raised on the third day according to the Scriptures.
1 Corinthians 15:3–4

I had known about God as a child. Like many cultures and faiths, families follow the traditions of their parents. I did this. In earlier stories, I speak about how I went through different stages of the development of my faith—as I am still doing—from accepting the truth I had heard as a child in church to making my own choice to become a Jesus follower, which involved layers of understanding.

This was another one of them.

It was just before Easter. As Jesus's followers, Easter is foundational to our faith. The local movie theatre was to show the Jesus movie. In preparation for this, some of the students from the Bible college in the midlands of England went door to door, inviting people to come to see it. I sat in the back row of the theatre thinking I knew all this stuff, but when the scene of Jesus crucified on the cross came, it hit my heart in a way I least expected it to. This truth was not only in the Bible that Christians believed or that only bad people needed to hear. He did this for me. I deserved to go to hell, and Jesus made a way so I didn't have to go. It was like hearing it for the first time.

I came out of the theatre unable to speak, never said a word on the car ride home, and once back at the college, just wept. I fell on my knees, saying repeatedly, "I'm so sorry for my sin that put You there, and thank You, thank You, thank You."

It was a solemn moment that changed my life forever.

I still had so much to learn and would spend the rest of my life in awe of His great love for all the world.

Reflection:

1. We need to find God for ourselves to own what we believe truly.
2. Don't settle with a weak faith in God. Pursue Him and discover who He is.

This Is the Role I Have for You

I will instruct you and teach you in the way you should go; I will counsel you with my loving eye on you.
Psalm 32:8

You will go out in joy and be led forth in peace.
Isaiah 55:12a

I was back in New Zealand after three years overseas in Australia, the Philippines, and then England. Now that I am home, what should I do? I needed to work to have money, or I would keep living at home. Plus, all my friends had left this seaside town.

I decided to drive to Wellington to see my best friend. I went for two interviews: hotel receptionist and office junior. I could have got them both, but there was no peace of mind. Driving back home to Napier, my peace returned. The circumstances had not changed; I still had no job, but I was convinced that God had it in His hands.

I joined a new church and began serving in the background.

I worked as a nurse aide on night duty at a Salvation Army rest home. I went to work at 10.30 pm and left my work every morning at 7.00 am. It was wintertime, so I never saw the light of day. I was miserable. I remember praying, Lord, please show me how to do the best I can at this job so I can move on.

Three months later, the minister asked me to pray about becoming a youth leader for the six teenagers they had in the church. I was 24 years old without a clue how to relate to teenagers.
Finally, it was my day off. Due to working nights for three months, I could not sleep. As I was talking to the Lord about the possible job, a thought from God came to my mind: "This is the role I have for you." Immediately, peace and joy filled my heart. I would accept the job.
God blessed the job, and within six months, the group grew from six kids to 60. During that time, I also completed an on-the-job two-year youth pastor diploma with the Baptist Union.

Reflection:
1. Do you think that, if you surrender your life to God, He has a specific job for you to do?
2. Can you see patterns in your own life where God is very clearly leading you—times when you made decisions, and times when you let God make them for you?
3. If you want "the A plan" for your life, how can you make that happen?

God Can Handle It

How long must I wrestle with my thoughts and day after day have sorrow in my heart? How long will my enemy triumph over me?
Psalm 13:2

I returned to New Zealand without a husband, not even engaged. I felt like such a failure. I was 24 years old with friends from my youth group and home church who were married (and some with children). These friends organised a youth group reunion to share my adventures far and wide.

I should have been grateful, but all I could think about was where I would position myself in those awkward group photos where everyone had a spouse except me.

They loved my modern European clothes and new haircut and almost seemed envious of all the travel I had done, but my heart was still so broken over my breakup with John.

I did the part, smiled, and laughed at the appropriate times, but I was only living on the surface. Underneath, I was angry. I was angry at God for allowing this to happen to me.

I did a youth pastors course with the Baptist Union at home. I would go away for a few weeks to study with others. One evening, one of the staff invited me for a walk along the beach. I think she knew something wasn't right. I was distant, even when I loved the program so much.

It was evening, so it was dark outside. This darkness gave me a freedom that I wasn't expecting. I soon started reliving John's and my nine-month courtship. The woman with me encouraged me to speak aloud about my feelings. I had never shared in this way with anyone before, but as I got into it, there was a marvellous release. I forgot she was beside me; instead, I got angry with God and let Him have it.

At first, this seemed wrong, but then I felt He was encouraging me to say it as it was. Instead of being struck by lightning, God felt closer than ever before. He was right in the midst of my pain. He was listening; He was aching with me. I fell on my knees and told Him I was sorry for holding onto this.

At the end of the walk, I felt much lighter. It was as if I had been carrying the weight of bitterness, anger, and sorrow—and it was no longer a weight for me to carry alone. I could give it to God.

The world was colourful again; I was free, forgiven for being angry, and comforted through God's deep compassion for me.

Reflection:

1. Do you need to be honest with God? Tell Him exactly how you feel about something. In Psalm 13, you see David speaking honestly to God.
2. Can you see how God can handle you being honest with Him and give you comfort and healing from any pain you've experienced?

Nothing Good Ever Happens to Me

If you, then, though you are evil, know how to give good gifts to your children, how much more will your Father in heaven give good gifts to those who ask him!
Matthew 7:11 [14]

Do you ever feel like all you do is work to please God? On one side, you know He deserves all of who we are. He's so worthy of all our time, but some days, it doesn't feel like that.

One of those days, feeling sorry for myself, I was thinking, "I'm always working and doing good things for other people. I live with four other single women who have 'normal' jobs and seem to do anything they want whenever they want to do it. Why is it so different for me?"

I was a youth pastor at the time with endless things to do. The phone kept ringing; I ran a Bible study in our house for 35 teenagers; parents needed advice, and there were fun activities to organise every Saturday night. I loved it, but I just wanted something nice to happen to me.

That is when it happened.

I heard a cat crying outside our back door. I grew up with cats. They have always brought me so much joy over the years. I opened the door, and there he was. He came bounding in like he owned the place. He was very vocal and affectionate. I fed him, and you can guess what happened. He stayed. I decided to call him "Toby," which means God is good. Saying the cat's name would remind me that God is good. I repented of my self-pity party and thanked God for this gift.

Reflection:

1. Do you ever feel this way?
2. What do you do when others seem to have it better off than you?
3. Can we trust God to care for our wants and our needs?

14 Jesus said these words.

Taking the Blame

Take my yoke upon you and learn from me, for I am gentle and humble in heart, and you will find rest for your souls. For my yoke is easy and my burden is light.
Matthew 11:29–30 [15]

It's all my fault! She would have never gotten into this car accident if I hadn't asked her to help us. She could still be a dancer. I didn't deserve her forgiveness. I ruined her life.

Lucy was recommended to me by a dancer friend who was more than happy to help the youth group. I wanted to put a musical together for a performance at the Teen Convention, where youth groups all over New Zealand would compete.

There was such a buzz in the air as we did auditions, had costumes made, and spent endless hours rehearsing all the dances Lucy showed us. We had a good chance of winning; we knew it.

I hired a coach; we set off for a five-hour journey from Napier to Wellington. It would be epic. We would come home with stories to tell and a trophy. Lucy and her husband said they wanted to drive their car there, and we were to meet at the church hall where we were staying.

We'd saved them dinner and started to worry about where they were. They should have been there by now. Then the phone rang to tell us they were in a horrific car accident; Lucy was heading to surgery. She had broken her hip and lower leg in a few places and was barely conscious.

The accident happened around Dannevirke, which was early in the trip. Lucy was in a large hospital near Dannevirke, so that we couldn't see her until our journey back to Napier.

I went to see her, but she didn't want to see me. She needed someone to blame because the doctor said she would never dance again. I took all that guilt onboard. Once home from the convention (which we didn't win, unfortunately), I could only beat myself up. I couldn't eat or sleep and didn't know what

15 Jesus said these words.

to do with this burden of ruining her life.

Lucy took months to recover and now walked with a limp. I asked if I could see her. Nevertheless, when I got there to ask her forgiveness, she said she could never do that.

What would I do with this enormous weight of guilt? There was only one thing I could do; I needed to give in to my Lord; I needed to let myself off the hook. It wasn't my fault. I wasn't driving the truck that hit them, nor their car. I couldn't carry this for the rest of my life. I was deeply sorry it had happened; still, I needed to let it go.

I got on my knees and surrendered this to God and asked Him to help me leave it with Him.

Reflection:

1. Have you ever gone through something like this—when you have taken all the blame for something that you really could have done nothing about?

2. God doesn't want you to carry that. We aren't living in heaven yet, so bad things still happen. Pray a simple prayer in your own words and give it to God.

Powerful Turn-Around

May the Lord answer you when you are in distress;
may the name of the God of Jacob protect you.
Psalm 20:1

I had been home in NZ for two years and led a youth group in my home church. In my last year leading the group, I made many bad decisions to prove I was lovable after being rejected by a group of friends. I got into the wrong friendship; what started as a fruitful ministry soon dropped in number due to me taking control of my life.

One evening, God and I had a long talk when I felt desperately alone. I had not been spending time with Him; He seemed a million miles away. I simply cried as I poured my heart out to Him. I asked Him to forgive me for all the wrong choices. I needed to forgive those who had hurt me at the beginning of this story and asked God to forgive me for holding that against them. Lastly, and most importantly, I completely surrendered my life again to God, telling Him that I would only follow in His ways for me.

I went to bed and fell into a deep sleep, only to be woken to what felt like my face was being forced into my pillow and something on top trying to suffocate me. In a muffled voice as though under a pillow, I yelled out twice, "Jesus, Jesus," and it lifted off me. My head rose again to a natural position on the pillow. Satan was not thrilled with my earlier conversation with God. He had tried to frighten me with this tactic, but it had not worked. Jesus's name had saved me.

The Bible tells us this. John, a disciple of Jesus, reminds the church in his letter, "The one who is in you is greater than the one who is in the world" (1 John 4:4). In John chapter 17 (Jesus's prayer before He leaves this world), He prays for His followers to be safe from the evil one.

Reflection:

1. What do you do to get back on track with God?
2. Think about how powerful the name of Jesus is. Have you ever seen it working in your life or in the life of others? In the Bible we see we don't have to fear Satan, as Jesus defeated him at the cross. Don't let fear stop you from doing things for God.

Can Anything Good Come Out of the Book of Leviticus?

Create in me a pure heart, O God, and re-
new a steadfast spirit within me.
Psalm 51:10

I was on a team in downtown Auckland, New Zealand, offering prayer to anyone who asked for it. We were in front of the church on a busy street. People would stop and ask for prayer for all sorts of things; we were happy to pray for them.

Our team leader had an idea for us to read the Bible out loud over a speaker for three days and simply let the power of God's Word speak to people.

As many of you know, the first five books of the Bible are called the Torah and are read by Jews, Christians, and Muslims. Moses wrote these books, inspired by God. Leviticus is a practical book written with many rules on how to live your life in those times.

While someone was reading from the Bible in Leviticus, Lillian, a 72-year-old woman, walked by the church. I was standing near her; therefore, she came to me. Lillian had been listening and heard the word unclean.

Desperately, she wailed, "I'm unclean. Show me how to become clean." I had the privilege of sharing my faith with her and telling her what Jesus did to make her clean. She left in peace.

Reflection:

1. What can you learn about the power of God's Word?
2. If all of the Bible is God-inspired, can He use any of it to speak to us in our particular circumstances?
3. What did Jesus do to make us clean?

A Brief Encounter with Heaven

For God so loved the world that he gave his one and only Son, that whoever believes in him shall not perish but have eternal life.
John 3:16

My father had two significant encounters with God that I remember well. Many of us wonder about what heaven is like; my father went there after a near-death experience.

At 21 years old, my father had an accident that changed his life. He fell down a 50-foot cargo hold on a navy ship after serving in World War II. My mother was a nurse in the hospital near where the ship was anchored, in Wellington harbour. When he came in, he was left in a side room to die. The doctor said, "He will be dead soon." My mother felt she needed to pray for him.

He did die, but only for a few seconds. In that short time, he recalls he went to heaven and heard beautiful choirs singing. He wanted to go in but sensed he wasn't able to. He pleaded to God, "I promise to follow after You, Jesus, just let me live. I'll do whatever You want me to." He suddenly came back to life.

He married my mother and went on their honeymoon at a Christian conference. There, he gave his life to God and became a Jesus follower. Sadly, money became his first love after living with little money and struggling to find a job. Around the time I was born in the early 60s, he had a good job.

As I grew older, I regularly prayed with my mother for my father to return to our Lord. In 1990, my parents sold the back of our property to a land developer, as it was getting too much for them to manage.
A young man of 17 years old who was a carpenter and a Christian came every day to build on the land. After many conversations with my father, the young man challenged him, especially after he gave my father a verse (Mark 8:36) from the holy Scriptures, in which Jesus said, "What good is it for someone to gain the whole world, yet forfeit their soul?"
My father later told me he kept thinking about that and had a long conversation with God, recommitting his life to Him. He died a year later in 1991.

Reflection:
1. Are you ready to meet your maker? That's a rather blunt question; still in this story, you can see my father was not. God gave him a second and a third chance to make that right.
His brief encounter with life after death showed him (and me) there was more to living a good life here on earth. We need to believe in why Jesus came and make it right with Him before we would be able to enter heaven.
My father's life changed dramatically in a moment, from being a carefree 21-year-old to dying after an accident. Life can be so unpredictable.
2. Think about what you may need to do to be ready to die.

A Gracious God Helps a Disorganised Follower

David also said to Solomon his son, "Be strong and courageous, and do the work. Do not be afraid or discouraged, for the Lord God, my God, is with you. He will not fail you or forsake you."
1 Chronicles 28:20

I've always been bad at finding out all the details of exactly where I need to go. This time was no exception; I was heading to Germany for the first time. I only had a ticket to Frankfurt, which was cheaper than going straight to Hamburg.

I got a taxi to the address I had in my purse from my flight, only to find out it was just an office of the Bible college in Frankfurt. They were very kind; I was able to fax the Hamburg office to find out if they were expecting me and how to get there.

It took a long time to get a reply. Finally, a fax came to the office saying one car in Frankfurt was leaving today for Hannover. I still needed to catch a train to Hamburg from Hannover, which they were happy to help me with.

Once I got to Hamburg, my only address was the office downtown in a red-light district. It was now 11 pm. On the office door was a sign in German—Open at 9 am.

I sat on the steps at the bottom of the office door and figured I would have to sleep there till morning. I was terrified. Unfamiliar with the nightlife and with all kinds of folks around me, I wrapped myself around my suitcase and began to cry. Lord, I need You.

A few minutes later, one of the staff from the college who lived nearby decided to return to the office to get something for the next day. She was shocked to see me there but happily insisted I come with her to stay the night. God did answer a seemingly impossible prayer when I desperately needed Him to.

Reflection:

1. I love how gracious God is when He's working with me, an unprepared kid, yet still comes through to help me when I mess it up. Can you see this kind of caring God through this story?
2. A simple prayer like, Lord, I need You, may be all that one needs to pray.
3. Can you remember when you were desperate for His help, and He answered your prayer? Believe He can do it again.

Creation Groans

The fool says in his heart, "There is no God."
Psalm 14:1

There is NO God, and if there was, He is dead."
For many years, parts of Europe suffered under the hands of communism. It was a terrible time in many ways. In schools at a very young age, children were brainwashed to believe that God was dead and that He could never help them. Christians had been praying for years for the "Iron Curtain," as it was known, to come down.
In 1989, God was about to change things in Europe, because He was alive and still is. I was in Australia then, in one of the many prayer groups worldwide, praying for God to move through Europe. The Berlin Wall came down in November 1989, and finally, we could take the good news of Jesus to a people who had never heard about Him. I joined an outreach to walk and pray through East Germany.
When we first crossed from West Germany to East Germany, we deeply yearned to praise God. And not just us: it felt like all the creation around us wanted to, as well. There was no wind before we crossed the border, and when we crossed, it blew. The trees moved their branches like arms praising God. It reminded me of the people waving palm branches leading up to Easter Sunday to usher in Jesus on a donkey. The cows and sheep came to the fences, unafraid of us, to say, "You are here at last!"
It's hard to explain, but it was as the Scripture says: "The whole creation has been groaning" for Him (Romans 8:22). [16]
We had arrived in this barren land, which had claimed for years that there was no God, and we had brought Him with us. This part of the earth was waking up to the truth of God being alive and was rejoicing because of it. We began to call

[16] A letter to the church in Rome from a church leader.

out to God that the people of this land would be rejoicing, too, just as creation had when it awoke to His presence.

Reflection:
1. What do you think of this quote? "Becoming an atheist is not through people's careful consideration of the facts, but by refusing to accept what the facts all around them are saying" (unknown author).
2. Take a moment to pray for people you know who don't have faith in God.

God in the Ordinary Things

Take delight in the Lord, and he will give you the desires of your heart.
Psalm 37:4

It was the first summer after the Berlin Wall had come down: July 1990. I had joined a small team to pray and walk through the former east part of Germany. We started in Hamburg and went to Nuremberg via Berlin and Dresden—900 km. We would walk 30 km a day, sleeping in the forest or a hall and sometimes in people's homes. The one in front walked with a wooden cross on a wheel leaning on his shoulder, and the last person would pray for 15 minutes. Then we would change places. We would stop every hour for water and chocolate, and then, typically, we would have sandwiches for lunch.

One particular day, I dreamed of roast chicken with gravy and vegetables. I mentioned it to the one walking beside me. It was ridiculous to think of this, as it could never happen.

We came to a small village, and like so many places, people would come running out to greet us or give us food for the journey. This time, a man said, "Please come with us and have lunch." He led us to a factory canteen and asked us to sit down. Soon, someone placed lunch before us. You guessed it. It was roast chicken, gravy, and vegetables.

Reflection:

1. What do you learn about God in this story?
2. If God has no favourites, can He do something like this for you?
3. Can you trust Him not only for your needs but for your wants and desires?

Pre-Conditioned

But the Lord said to Samuel, "Do not consider his appearance or his height, for I have rejected him. The Lord does not look at the things people look at. People look at the outward appearance, but the Lord looks at the heart."
1 Samuel 16:7

3 October 1990 was to be the day of remembrance for the reunification of the two Germanys: East and West coming together. We held a service especially for this.

God had prepared my heart for Germany through prayer in Australia and East Germany on the first prayer walk I attended after it opened. The wall between East and West Germany came down in November 1989 as parts of Europe were opening up to allow freedom of religion, and the grip of communism was losing its hold.

What I didn't expect was how my mind had been brainwashed. I had only ever seen the Germans as the enemy through movies, stories of my father fighting in the war, and other propaganda. So, when I looked around in the service, I was astounded by what I thought I saw. In my mind, I saw everyone sitting in army uniform. I had to blink twice to get past it.

One by one, people arose from their seats to share what the two Germanys becoming one had meant to them. It was very moving. At times, there weren't many dry eyes in the room. A young man shared how he had always been so ashamed to be known as a German because of the country's history, and he found it hard to be proud of the recent win of the World Cup Series in soccer. I was moved by what he said and spoke to him afterwards. I felt like I represented those who held him back in the past from being proud of who he was. I asked his forgiveness for my attitude and judgements. He thanked me, but I realised it broke something in me, and I never looked back.

From that day on, I chose to speak proudly of my young German friends and defend them against others' prejudiced words or actions. My voice for them developed even more as the years went on, as I looked into some beautiful history they were part of before both world wars. It also opened me up to see how God sees this nation.

Reflection:

1. Do you feel challenged by strong negative views towards a group of people?
2. How do you feel when someone has prejudiced thoughts towards you?
3. Is it something you can invite God into to change your heart?

Confirming I'm in the Right Place (Language School, Part 1)

I will instruct you and teach you in the way you should go;
I will counsel you with my loving eye upon you.
Psalm 32:8

Now in Germany, I needed to learn the language. It would be challenging, but if this was where I felt I should be, I would need to work at it. I used to wake up hoping the words would flow out of my mouth. Unfortunately, there was no easy road, so I needed to attend language school. I had no money to get the bus there, nor to pay for school, and there were holes in the only boots I possessed; but I knew if God were on my side, I would get there somehow.

Nearly all the money came in for the first month of the school from some friends who felt led to give it without me saying I needed it. I still needed 81 Deutschmarks (£36), plus bus money.

I said nothing to anyone, just to God. I knew I should prepare as though I was going, so I went to the basement to iron my outfit.

While I was ironing, one of the staff came down to find me. He said, "I felt God wanted to give you my tithe for this month; it's 81 Deutschmarks."

God had very specifically answered my prayer. I floated up the stairs as if on "cloud nine." When I returned to my room, my roommate gave me paper and pens for class. I just needed the bus fare to get there.

The next day, I woke up ready to go in my freshly pressed clothes, still with no money for the bus. Just as I was about to leave, another staff member came running down the stairs with the bus fare for a month. I was overwhelmed with joy as I walked to the bus stop, knowing God had prompted people to help me when I didn't have a visa to work here. He was in this, and I was in the right place.

Reflection:

1. Remind yourself of God being in the details of your life when no one has any idea you need anything.
2. Can you believe He will do it again if He's done it before?

Don't Presume (Language School, Part 2)

Trust in the Lord with all your heart and lean not on your understanding; in all your ways submit to him, and he will make your paths straight.
Proverbs 3:5–6

Three months was the recommended amount of time to go to language school. I had seen the money come in for the first two months, so there was no reason why God wouldn't come through for another month.

The time was getting close to paying for it. I thought it must be on its way, so I'd help God out and pay the deposit with my credit card. God would sort it out. Three months was the recommended time, but nothing came in.

I bought the bus fare with my credit card and went. I had no peace or joy this time, just determination. I was walking up the stairs to the classroom when I believed the Lord put in my mind, "What are you doing here!?"

It came across in a way that I instantly realised I had done this in my strength. Like a dog with its tail between its legs, I went to the office and told the head teacher I had to leave and shouldn't be there this month. The deposit was non-refundable. She didn't understand, but I knew I needed to go. God did not want me here this month. I turned and left to take the bus back to where I was staying. I told God how sorry I was for insisting on my way when it was clear there was no extra money given to the school to confirm this was what He wanted for me. My place is to follow Him, not the other way around.

It was a harsh lesson, but I needed to obey Him in this, as who knows what He'd ask me to do in the future? I wanted Him to know He could trust me to follow through when it mattered.

Reflection:

1. Why does following God all the time matter?
2. Can you see in your life the times things went wrong when you did them your way?

Unlikely Choice

Moses said to the Lord, "Pardon your servant, Lord. I have never been eloquent, neither in the past nor since you have spoken to your servant. . . . The Lord said to him, "Who gave human beings their mouths? . . . Is it not I, the Lord? Now go; I will help you speak and will teach you what to say."
Exodus 4:10–12

"Who? Me? You must have made a mistake!"

I had been in Hamburg, Germany, for only three months, with no grip on the language and only the word of the Lord to come here.

It was time to elect a new leader to run one of the Bible schools. There was no likely candidate. We prayed, and the team leader felt we should put names forward, and if the same name came up three times, this was the one God chose.

It was my name that came up three times.

I gasped and looked around at smiling faces. In my mind, I thought, That can't be right. Immediately, the team leader said, "This must be God," and prayed over me.

I returned to my room full of doubt and fell on my knees. "God, what are You doing? You know I can't do this; I'm so inadequate." As I waited on God, full of anxiety, a beautiful peace settled in my heart. He was in this, and we would do this together.

The guy who had been running the school had burnt out, so he wasn't able to help me at all, but God provided Renate as my "right-hand lady." She was so gifted and helped me set up the school. It was to be a bilingual English/German school. God also provided an exceptional translator who translated my every word.

God stood beside me, a poorly educated girl who could barely communicate in German, to lead a wonderful group of students and staff.

Reflection:

1. Has God ever called you to do something that you felt inadequate to do?
2. Take a moment to remember how it went. What did you learn from the experience?
3. Is He asking you to trust Him again to do something new for Him?
4. Even a great man like Moses felt inadequate (see the verse at the top). Does this reassure you?

God Can Prepare Us

Now the Lord provided a huge fish to swallow Jonah, and Jonah was in the belly of the fish three days and three nights.
Jonah 1:17

I never could fill the hole in my heart. I ate to try and fill it, even when I wasn't hungry. I slept so I didn't have to think about it. I isolated myself so I didn't have to hear people's comments and condolences.

It was my 27th birthday, and I had been walking back from the train station to the Bible school where I was working in Germany when I heard the Lord say, "Your father is going to die soon." Wow, that was hard. I was not expecting Him to say that, but I knew He had. I went straight to my room and planned to return to New Zealand.

My father wasn't sick, and he was only 63 years old, but I felt I would not be home when he died, so I needed to prepare the way for when it happened.

Once home in New Zealand, I saw two elders from my church. I told them exactly the way I had heard it from God: "I believe my dad is going to die soon."

The first gentleman I visited laughed, shrugged his shoulders in disbelief, and said, "No, he's fine." The second one nodded sincerely. I asked him and his wife to be there for my mother. They gave a solemn look and agreed they would.

Four weeks later, after I had returned to Germany, my father died of a blood clot from his heart that went to his brain and caused a massive stroke. Of course, it was hard to lose my father, but God's warning allowed me one final visit with him, and I'll always treasure the memory of that.

Reflection:

1. What can I learn from this story?
2. If you were in this story, who would you be—the doubting elder, or the one who believed?

He Goes Before Us

The lions may grow weak and hungry,
but those who seek the Lord lack no good thing.
Psalm 34:10

Have you ever arrived at midnight in Calcutta, India (with a 5 am departure scheduled from New Delhi the following day) only to discover no accommodation was arranged for you?

My travel agent hadn't considered the layover, and I was unsure where I would sleep at the Calcutta airport. I was so tired from my flight from Germany, but God had already devised a plan to sort this all out.

I went to fetch my bags as if on automatic, dazed from the long flight. A taxi driver tried to get my attention, but I didn't speak the language. Then the only white man in sight approached me, saying, "Are you okay?" He had just flown back to Calcutta from NZ and was on his way home. After chatting for a while, we discovered we both had the same faith and worked for the same international organisation. He offered to take me home to his family so I could rest and return to the airport in the morning.

It was my first time in India, and I knew nothing about the culture. As we drove through the streets, the poverty was overwhelming and heart-breaking. This man and his family had started a company to help women come out of prostitution. He had a team of women show them

how to sew shopping bags and other items to give them an alternate trade. Someone distributed this sewing worldwide, and whenever he travelled overseas, he would take more bags with him to sell, and the money would go back to the women.
As I settled in for the night, I smiled at how God had a New Zealander at the airport when I arrived, as He already knew I needed accommodation even before I did.

Reflection:
1. Can you see God in this story?
2. What would you have done when you found out you had nowhere to rest before your next flight in a strange country?
3. Does this verse from the holy Scriptures bring you comfort?

Ducks, a Tree, and Snow

If you remain in me and my words remain in you, ask whatever you wish, and it will be done for you.
John 15:7 [17]

This Christmas had the potential to be the worst Christmas ever. My father had died 18 months earlier, and I had no money. I didn't have paid work, as I was volunteering at a Bible school in Germany.

I lived in a flat with three others I didn't know well. They had also decided to stay because they couldn't afford to go home (and other reasons).

We lived in the middle of nowhere. The buildings were built deliberately as a factory for making weapons during World War II. Trees acted as camouflage over all the buildings we lived in to stop the factory building from being seen by the enemy. Only a few knew we were there. There were no shops for miles, just open fields across from us. We were living in the former staff quarters, which were warm and comfortable. We watched as students and staff left for the holidays. How could this situation ever improve? One of the roommates suggested we come together and pray. It wasn't something I was in the mood to do at all. She recommended we discuss what we would like for Christmas, then bring our resources together and see what God would do. One said they wanted a decorated Christmas tree; another said two ducks for the main course; and I said I would love it to snow on Christmas Eve. We gave our desires to God. Some had faith it would happen, but I felt it was like writing a list for Father Christmas to answer, with little chance it would happen.

I left the room worried about having bread and jam for Christmas Day lunch.

My friend Chris said she was leaving the next day and her family had sent her a decorated Christmas tree; would we like it? One of us received a gift of money

17 Jesus said these words.

and bought two ducks with all the trimmings. And—you guessed it—it snowed on Christmas Eve just as we left for the midnight service. God knew where we lived—even if we were tucked away from the rest of the world—and heard our hearts' desires.

Reflection:

1. When you pray, do you think God only cares about our needs, or could He even care about our desires?
2. What is your best memory of God coming through for you when you least expected it?

It Is Finished

Martha opened her home to him. She had a sister called Mary, who sat at the Lord's feet listening to what he said. But Martha was distracted by all the preparations that had to be made. She came to him and asked, "Lord, don't you care that my sister has left me to do the work by myself? Tell her to help me!" "Martha, Martha," the Lord answered, "you are worried and upset about many things, but few things are needed—or indeed only one. Mary has chosen what is better, and it will not be taken away from her."
Luke 10:38b–42

Jesus said, "It is finished." With that, he bowed his head and gave up his spirit.
John 19:30b

I was in Germany at the time when three words changed my life. Although my name is Mary, I think I've been a Martha. Mary felt secure in Jesus's love for her, so that she could sit at His feet and simply listen to Him. Martha was always doing things. Like most of us, she thought that was the right thing to do.

It was the evening of the community meeting (like a midweek church service). I was hosting the evening, so my thoughts were racing with all I needed to do—make sure the guest speaker had what she needed, and that we had made enough cakes to serve everyone after the service—when I heard her say, "IT IS FINISHED."

It startled me. I thought she meant the meeting had finished, and I wasn't nearly ready. I listened more intently. What is finished?

She spoke about how Jesus was born into a time when Jews followed the laws every day: rituals like washing, ways of preparing food, etc., to make you clean and holy to fulfil the laws of Moses. Jesus came to complete the law and bring it to its fulfilment. She meant we could be completely free to live, due to Him dying on the cross and fulfilling all prophecies.

The message from Jesus always seemed too simple. Especially with the life I had lived, I needed to do more to earn my way to heaven. We don't need to "do" things to pay our way to heaven. Our motivation needs to simply be to serve Him because we love Him because of all He did for us. IT IS FINISHED, was His final cry. These three words finally hit my heart. What she said made me realise He was talking to me.

Reflection:

1. What motivates you to serve God?
2. Can you believe He is happy for you to just sit at His feet?
3. How do we stay in that place?

Food That Lasts

Jesus answered, "Everyone who drinks this water will be thirsty again, but whoever drinks the water I give them will never thirst."
John 4:13–14a

It would be the craziest journey I had ever made: five days by train from Moscow to Chita, Siberia. It had been an unproductive harvest, and now the long winter lay before them. Many villages in this part of Siberia had very little to eat. A group of students from the Bible school in Germany decided to go by train and take German food to them.

I was in between projects, so I volunteered to go with them. Chita had had a long, harsh winter, and the autumn reserves ran out. God reminded me how blessed I was to have an abundant supply of food whenever I needed it.

We packed ten banana-sized boxes of cheese, sausage, tinned fish and vegetables, etc. Anything full of preservatives with a long life.

Riding third class meant we had exciting people to share the space with, including livestock. Chickens in cages stared at dogs on leads tied to the ends of bottom bunk beds. Mattresses too big for the beds overhung them. Fully bearded men smoked and dropped ash in their beards; large Babushkas laughed and squeezed small children.

We travelled to the far side of Russia, from Moscow to Novosibirsk, through Irkutsk and over the frozen Lake Balal to Ulan-Ude.

We stayed with families who offered us fantastic hospitality. Homes were heated with coal, which is surprisingly very effective. Although it was -30 degrees outside, inside, you were pretty warm.
Our team gave out the boxes of food we had brought with us, but of course, due to their generosity, the families insisted we eat their food. Each family had an Oma, the oldest lady in the house. It was so cold downstairs in the cellar, under the house; refrigeration was unnecessary. She would bring up meat—mainly fat with a bit of meat attached, and a jar of apples to prepare a meal with potatoes.
This village had recently heard about Jesus, so they requested us to come and share about Him and God. The physical food we brought them wouldn't last forever, but the story of Jesus coming to quench our deepest thirst would. Invitations went out to schools, hospitals, and town halls for people to come to hear about God through a translator. Passionately, we shared what we believed from the Bible.

Reflection:
1. Do you find yourself trying to fill your unhappiness with things that only satisfy you briefly?
2. We often say we have a God-sized hole in us that only God can fill. I believe that. We can try to fill it with overeating and other addictions, but they will never satisfy us fully. If we believe God created us, surely He knows how to help us best.

Not Alone

Have I not commanded you? Be strong and courageous. Do not be afraid, do not be discouraged, for the Lord your God will be with you wherever you go.
Joshua 1:9

It was my 30th birthday. I have a tradition on all my birthdays: I like to take time away from any celebrations and have time alone with God. For years, I've been afraid and cautious about some bad things that have happened to me. I still struggle to walk alone day or night, especially in an unknown area.

I wanted to stroll to focus on God, but this place wasn't familiar. I was in a bit of a dilemma as I stood on the edge of the driveway of the property. Suddenly, a large, black, scary dog, like a Rottweiler, stood beside me. I had never seen him before; he simply came out of nowhere.

As I studied him a little more, I saw one side of his lip go up in one corner, almost like he was trying to give me a smile. His gentle eyes reassured me to relax. When I moved even just a little bit, he moved, too. I decided to test him, and slowly, I left the property. He stayed with me for the entire time, for at least a couple of miles, as I talked and listened to God. I was even relaxed enough to enjoy the walk. He accompanied me back to where I was staying and then left. I don't know in which direction he went, for as quickly as he appeared, he was gone.

Reflection:

1. Things may have happened in your past that have brought fear into your life. Like in this story, I believe God can provide for you so you can step out again and enjoy your life.

Step by Step

The Lord makes firm the steps of the one who delights in him; though he may stumble, he will not fall, for the Lord upholds him with his hand.
Psalm 37:23–24

I was to return to New Zealand. My Lord had made this very clear to me on my last visit home; my time in Germany was over. I had no idea where I would live in NZ, but I knew if this were God's idea, He would have a plan.

One of our most recent staff at the college, Sally, came from Christchurch, NZ. Her minister came to see her. I thought to myself, Christchurch would be a nice place to live and work. There are tourists there; I could speak German. Meeting this minister meant this could be a potential church I could attend; it all started to sound good.

Sally had arranged for someone from the church to pick me up at the airport and for me to stay with her mother. The lady needed to drop by her church first. I went straight to the church notice board where I saw an advert: "A female housemate wanted," with contact details. I wrote it down, then asked where the house was, and she said it was within walking distance of this church. It all sounded perfect.

Step by step, God was going before me and making a way. I had nothing to add to the house, as I only owned the clothes in my bag. The main person asking for a roommate had everything. Her parents even dropped a mattress over for me to sleep on till I got my own. I felt so welcome. I cried myself to sleep with a thankful heart for God's provision.

I needed to transition from living almost seven years in Germany. God even provided for this. Via a series of emails, I got in touch with a couple who only lived 45 minutes from Christchurch and who specialised in helping people with transition. They invited me to stay for the weekend on their farm. It was what I needed.

Reflection:

1. If God leads you to move away from where you are now, can you trust Him to provide somewhere to live?
2. If He's done this for you before, remind yourself of this and follow Him wherever He leads you. His will for your life is always better than what you could have come up with.

Fish Out of Water

"For my thoughts are not your thoughts, neither are your ways my ways," declares the Lord. "As the heavens are higher than the earth, so are my ways higher than your ways and my thoughts than your thoughts."
Isaiah 55:8–9

I should feel very comfortable here—after all, this group of people speak my language and come from the same ethnicity and culture—and yet I feel like a fish out of water, I thought.

I had just returned home to New Zealand from Germany, and I was miserable. I had been living there for almost seven years. It was home. I could speak the language, had set up a flat there, had friends, loved the food, and could even watch German TV and understand it.

To be able to come home, I had to get a suitcase, as I had given my one suitcase away. I thought I would never leave, and in my heart, I was content with this. My mother was even learning German in a high school night class to speak with her future grandchildren. But then God called me home. I didn't fully understand then; I simply followed His guidance.

Everything seemed new. I remember going to a small corner shop to buy something simple to eat and wanting to ask for it in German. This language has become so automatic to me.

I had to make new friends in New Zealand, go to a new church, buy things to be able to live—like a bed—and find a job, yet I was doing all this with grief in my heart over leaving Germany.
I knew God was with me, and I could talk to Him about how I felt anytime. I often cried myself to sleep, thinking this pain would never go away, but talking to God helped me know in time it would change.

Reflection:
1. Following God and His ways for our lives is not always easy, but I've never been disappointed with His ways for me. I may question them and moan, but He eventually melts my heart, and I know His wisdom is always best. Can you see this in your life?
2. God sees the big picture for our lives, and He chose just the right timing for me to leave Germany, as He didn't want me to be part of some excruciating things that happened six months after I left. Can you trust Him even when you disagree with His choices for you?

When His Favour Is on Us

For no word from God will ever fail.
Luke 1:37

But Noah found favour in the eyes of the Lord.
Genesis 6:8

I was back in NZ after living in Germany for seven years. What should I do now? I had a good knowledge of the German language and a good understanding of the people and their culture. New Zealand was often a place where they could come and visit. The hospitality industry would be an excellent workplace; I just needed a formal education.

A friend helped me put a CV together by exploring all the experience I had gained over the last seven years in Germany. I still had no formal training, so when a job opening came up, others would be more likely to get the job, so I enrolled in an evening adult learning class—as a hotel receptionist.

I drove past a hotel one evening and thought, "Wouldn't that be a nice place to work?" A week later, a position became available at this hotel for a part-time receptionist. I applied and got asked to come in for an interview.

I did all I could to prepare for the interview. I wore a suit I had bought at a discount shop and prayed. I had never worked in this line of work

before, so I had no experience, but God gave me favour in their eyes, and I got it.
When God wants you somewhere, He can make it happen. Nothing is impossible to Him.

Reflection:
1. I believe God can set up a job to work with the experience you have in life, even without a formal education. Don't be discouraged if finding a job is proving to be challenging. Be willing to get some training if needed, but don't doubt God. He can open doors that look impossible to go through.

An Appointed Time

Sarah became pregnant and bore a son to Abraham in his old age, at the very time God had promised him.
Genesis 21:2

My plan was to be married at 22 years old, have three children, a house, a garden, and live in New Zealand. None of that happened. I met a man at 22 years old in England, and although I tried to make it work, God showed me He was not in it. No, He had a whole different plan, which required me to wait till I was 38 years old before I would meet the man I was to marry.

Ten years earlier, at 28 years old, I was living and working in Germany, and I started to question God about my future, reminding Him where I lived and that I was still single. I felt the Lord said, "He will be a Canadian." I wrote this in my journal, and being in an international organisation, I assumed God would bring him to me in Germany.

Fast forward to me being 37 years old. I felt the Lord was leading me to go to Canada. There was a need in my organisation for someone to mentor the female staff in their 20s, and they chose me to do this. Just as I was leaving for the airport to Vancouver, I felt I should take my 1992 journal; I had no idea why.

On the 16 June 2002, I first met Jay—my Canadian husband-to-be. The journal I took with me was the journal in which I had written ten years earlier, "He will be a Canadian."

Reflection:

1. Joyce Meyer, a well-renowned writer and speaker, says waiting is like going to the doctor. You have an appointment, but you must wait until it's your turn.
2. Has God ever shown you something quite clearly a long time before it happens? Why do you think He does this?
3. What do you do while you are waiting?
4. If you are waiting for something now, is anything stopping you from trusting God to keep His word?

A Red Rose

For you created my inmost being; you knit me together in my mother's womb. I praise you because I am fearfully and wonderfully made.
Psalm 139:13–14a

Jesus answered, "Everyone who drinks this water will be thirsty again, but whoever drinks the water I give them will never thirst."
John 4:13–14a

No one ever gave those women a rose. They weren't on the streets to have kindness shown to them; instead, people like June were used and discarded after acts of selfishness. Men stole their innocence and dignity. I was living in downtown Vancouver: Commercial Drive, well-known for the women working the streets at night. We lived close to the "not so" beautiful ladies who were not high-class and mainly needed the money to keep their drug habits going.

On Friday nights, we would walk amongst these prostitutes and hand out roses. It was one of these evenings when I met June. June was older than most of the ladies. She said she needed to do this, as her pimp gave her no choice. Working the streets was the only job June had known. The look on her face when she received the rose was unbelief. The rose symbolised beauty, which her life on the street did not. Then she broke and smiled, and with tears in her eyes, she thanked me. I told her how Jesus saw her as beautiful as this red rose, and how He could make everything clean and new again. She found that too hard to believe. The rose represented so much beauty for June from Jesus, but she couldn't see how her life could change.

God can redeem anyone from anything and make all things new. June's life was similar to the story of the woman at the well in the gospel of John, chapter 4. Jesus gave her hope and offered her a new beginning. We all need a Saviour at some point, even when we may not realise it, and He can give us a new beginning. June didn't choose to receive that truth and give her life up then, but we pray she will one day.

Reflection:

1. One of Jesus's followers wrote these words to a church in Corinth: "Therefore, if anyone is in Christ, the new creation has come: The old has gone, the new is here" (2 Corinthians 5:17). Is any sin too big for God to forgive?

2. Do you know others who have said God couldn't forgive them? Why don't you pray for them? Pray they will see they are worthy of His forgiveness.

His Shield Was All Around Me

My God sent his angel, and he shut the mouths of the lions. They have not hurt me because I was found innocent in his sight.
Daniel 6:22a

Once a week, I took one Canadian coin (called a loony) and my driver's licence with me for identification to work with a charity called Mission Possible. Vancouver is the warmest part of Canada in the winter, so people struggling with life often end up on the streets there. Downtown Vancouver was where drug addicts, prostitutes, and people who were homeless for all kinds of reasons lived.

Each week, I would walk across town, passing these folks on the streets on my way to an outreach place where I would serve coffee, teas, and doughnuts and chat with those who came in. It was here where I met William (another story in this book).

I loved to do this, but I was pretty nervous, so I briskly walked there and back to the train station. I would pray the whole way and keep my gaze straight in front of me.

I looked so out of place, and yet no one bothered me. I had heard this story of someone needing to get from one side of the city to the other in a dangerous area of the world and how God covered them with a shield so it seemed like they were invisible. The person saw everything around him, but it was like no one saw him.

I wondered if that is what God did for me.

It helped me to relax and trust God with my journey there and back. I wanted to be there to show His love to everyone from all walks of life.

Reflection:
1. I believe God can do anything; do you?
2. In the Bible verse from Daniel at the top of the page, God closed the lion's mouth to protect him. What do you think of that story?

God of Second Chances

Because of the Lord's great love we are not consumed, for his compassions never fail. They are new every morning; great is your faithfulness.
Lamentations 3:22–23

William had been a lawyer, but now he was known as Willie, a "nobody" who lived on the streets of Vancouver. As I sat across from him at the table in the "drop-in" called Mission Possible, he told me his story. He had a family, a beautiful wife, and a lovely home that he had lost to gambling. The debtors came for money to pay off his debts, so the house sold right under his family's feet, and his wife and kids left him. He went to the casino to try his luck again. Over and over again, he lost. Left with no choices, he gambled off his watch, which his father gave him, and his only jacket. Having nowhere to sleep, he went to the streets, found a cardboard box, and slept under it.

Like me, you may think, That will never happen to me. I don't gamble. But I'm sure when William was a child, his mother never thought it would happen to him. A series of bad decisions led him down this path, so let's choose to remain humble and call on God regularly.

I told William about how Jesus loved him, even in the state he was in now: that His love was unconditional and unending and was there for him if he chose to reach out to Him.

Jesus's unconditional love is there for all of us, no matter what we have done with our lives. There is always a second chance at life with Him. Unconditional love is a compelling concept. It means love without strings attached, no conditions: full acceptance without question, no expectations to know and understand the holy books, and no need to earn our way to heaven through good deeds. It is a love no one else can offer.

It has taken me years to understand this concept of unconditional love, that even though I might be a "good person," I can never earn His love for me. It's simply just there.

Sadly, William did not feel worthy to receive His love then, but I hope he does one day and starts his life again.

The holy Scriptures—the Bible in the Christian faith—has stories of people having a second chance to get things right. Jonah tried going the other way, Samson tried to do things in his strength, and David committed adultery, and God gave them all another chance.

Reflection:

1. Look up the meaning of "unconditional" in a dictionary, see what it means, and think about God's love for you in this way.
2. Pray for anyone you know who has an addiction to something, that they would be free to live without it.

Never Far from God's Eyes

The Lord himself goes before you and will be with you; he will never leave you nor forsake you. Do not be afraid; do not be discouraged.
Deuteronomy 31:8

Unfortunate circumstances had left Adul deserted. His dear mother had fallen into hard times and worked on the streets. Her family disowned her. She did not know what to do when she found out she was pregnant. A friend told her of a kind family providing a home for unwanted children, educating them, teaching from the holy books, and preparing them for the future.

I joined a team going to Morocco from Canada to help at this home as it quickly became an orphanage. I met Abdul. He was now three years old and full of life. Abdul looked healthy and happy. The family had taken him on as their son. They had another seven kids, some their own and the others they had adopted when the children were abandoned at their doorstep.

Our team went to play with the kids, help with renovations around the buildings, and work in preparing the large garden for vegetables.

I saw how God showed His great love for Abdul and the other children there through this family's selfless act of love and obedience to move from America to provide this form of care for others. I was overwhelmed by God's kindness and mercy. It made me think of our unfortunate circumstances or greatest mistakes and how God never abandons us.

Reflection:

1. Can you see God in this story?
2. When you read this verse from the holy Scriptures at the top of this story, how does it make you feel?

Not This Month

Be still, and know that I am God.
Psalm 46:10a

We had NZ $1,200 come to us from our taxes, which we needed to help God with my getting pregnant. I could go for two IUI trials, which happen before an IVF. I was 41 years old, and time was not on my side. We were told to try six months on our own, then with hormonal tablets to increase the number of eggs ovulating each month. We were in the middle of the hormonal tablets when the money came in to speed it all along. It must be God.

I went for an internal scan to see if I was ready for the IUI this month.

"Sorry," was the word that came out of her mouth. "You've ovulated on the same side as last month, the one with the blocked fallopian tube."

I went home devastated. Usually, you ovulate alternately each month.

God, I don't understand. We have the money to pay for it. Why not?

At that moment, I looked up to our board, where I had put a postcard with the verse, "Be still, and know that I am God." I smiled, sighed a breath of release, and felt at peace that He had it all in His hands. I was so relaxed that it wouldn't happen this month.

We went out for our second wedding anniversary and conceived Joshua that night.

When I was seven weeks pregnant, I was called in for a scan to check all was well. I asked the person, "Can you see which ovary the egg released from?"
He said, "That's strange; your blocked side released an egg, and you got pregnant from that side." I smiled, knowing God wanted all the glory for making our baby. When the doctor says, Not this month, it's impossible, God says, Be still, and you watch what I can do!

Reflection:
1. Do you ever try and help God out? Sarah, Abraham's wife, did this when she had Abraham sleep with the maidservant Haggai to give them a son. God had promised that their descendants would be more than the stars, and it wasn't happening fast enough, so Sarah took matters into her own hands.
2. Whenever I'm not patient and try to help God, it never works out well; it always goes much better when I let Him lead.

Heartbeat

A furious squall came up, and the waves broke over the boat, so that it was nearly swamped. Jesus was in the stern, sleeping on a cushion. The disciples woke him and said to him, "Teacher, don't you care if we drown?" He got up, rebuked the wind and said to the waves, "Quiet! Be still!" Then the wind died down and it was completely calm.
Mark 4:37–39

It was the house group potluck dinner, and all I ate was a warmed-up tuna pasta. I knew it was not warm enough, even as I ate it. Why did I do that? I knew better. I was nine weeks pregnant. Everyone knows that in your first three months of pregnancy, you must be careful with what you eat. You don't eat reheated food, especially not fish.

Was I going to miscarry? Why did I do this to myself?

I was 42 years old. The odds were against me having this baby in the first place—my age and the fact that I only had one functioning fallopian tube. Plus, I might not have many eggs left. I couldn't mess this up. I was beside myself with worry. I went to bed to rest but couldn't settle. I screamed out to God, phoned friends to pray, and begged the doctor's surgery for a scan. They agreed to take me that afternoon. The doctor told me it was early, and we may not hear the heartbeat, but she would still try. I was absorbed by the monitor, watching for any sign of movement. Of course, I couldn't tell what was what, but then I heard it—his heartbeat. Tears rolled down my face. The crisis was over.

Reflection:

1. Do you think God can come into our fears and calm the storm? Think of a time when He has done this for you. God doesn't always do it the same way, but our testimonies are examples that He does come to help us when we need it.

2. If you need Him to come into something you are going through right now, be honest with Him and invite Him into it. If you don't need this, pass it on to someone else and share your story of His faithfulness to someone else.

Daydreaming Can Be Dangerous

You are my hiding place; you will protect me from trouble and surround me with shouts of deliverance.
Psalm 32:7

Another friend's wedding. How exciting! I was seven months pregnant and looking across to a wedding store at all the beautiful dresses when suddenly I drove into the back of a car waiting at the traffic lights.

The loud bang startled me out of my daydream. The front of the car was coming into my legs, and I couldn't move. My thoughts went straight to my unborn child. I can't feel the baby moving. What's happening? Did I . . .? God, NO, please let the baby still be alive.

Immediately, two people came to my aid, one a doctor and one a nurse, in the cars behind me. They saw I was pregnant. Firm, authoritative, and yet calming words came from their mouths. BREATHE, BREATHE, try to relax; help is on its way.

I remember trying hard to relax, but how could I? I needed to know if my baby was all right.

The ambulance arrived. Carefully, I was extracted from the car. Quickly, I was connected to a baby monitor to check on the baby. Contractions started; now, there was concern for my unborn child, so I went to the neonatal unit. The baby's heartbeat was strong, and soon the contractions stopped.

As I began to relax, the pain registered in other parts of my body. It was hard to breathe, and my sternum was so sore. It was as if I never noticed this before when my thoughts were only towards the wellbeing of my unborn, but now it was about me. I was rushed to the other end of the hospital and discovered I had cracked my sternum, plus bruising. My son was fine, and we were discharged from the hospital and told to sleep sitting upright while my sternum healed.

Reflection:

1. Can you see God in this story?
2. What was the first thing He provided?
3. Does the verse from the holy Scriptures at the top of the story bring you hope in difficult times?

I Didn't Think I'd Be Like This

Why, my soul, are you downcast? Why so disturbed within me? Put your hope in God, for I will yet praise Him, my Saviour and my God.
Psalm 42:5

I had wanted a baby for years. What was wrong with me? I used to manage international schools and their trips overseas, yet I didn't know how to stop him from crying. He was four weeks old, and I was 42 years old. I wasn't coping. Tears came so quickly. There was sleep deprivation, getting dressed at noon, and having him attached to me every few hours. I had known how to do most things in life, including leading people, but I had no idea what to do with this baby. Plus, God felt so far away, like He had abandoned me. My husband tried to help, but I didn't know what he could do.

We were strongly encouraged to put the baby in the corridor near our room so we could sleep, but then I worried all night if he was breathing or not. My closest friends had jobs and weren't in this stage of life. It was winter, cold and bleak, and it became dark early. I desperately wanted this train to stop and for me to get off and feel normal again.

Then the fridge broke down, and it felt like the final straw.

God had my midwife drop in on that day. She saw how low I was feeling and told me to make an appointment with the doctor. Fortunately, my doctor, who had known me for years, told me this wasn't my usual self

and prescribed an antidepressant tablet. I came home ashamed that I needed this, but my body needed help to recover from a hormonal imbalance called postnatal depression.
As my mother used to say, "Sometimes you simply need pills to solve medical ills."

Reflection:
1. Depression of any kind can be hard to accept. Don't beat yourself up about it. If you need help, go and get it.
2. If you don't need the help for yourself and someone else you know does, encourage them to go and speak to a doctor. It is nothing to be ashamed of.

Time to Serve Here

The Lord said to him, "Go back the way you came . . ."
1 Kings 19:15a

I had loved being a stay-at-home mum until Joshua was three and a half years old, but now it was all about to change.

Jay came home with the news that his work was sizing down. In New Zealand, restructuring means the last one employed is the first one they "let go." That was him. He had only been there half a year. What did this mean for us?

I wasn't keen to return to serving God at a Bible college, but if we could stay in NZ, that might be easier. We went to see one of our Bible colleges, a 40-minute drive from where we lived. Something began to happen in my heart again to want to help others understand the Bible. While there, we made inquiries about where to rent a house.

After hearing of a family that wanted to rent out their place for two years, we went to look at it. It was a small farm eight kilometres from the college. We agreed to take it.

It was all happening very fast. In the early hours of the following morning, when neither Jay nor I could sleep, we held hands and prayed: "If this is Your will for us, please provide everything we need to do this."

The next day, a friend came and told me that she had the impression from God in prayer that she should give us part of the ten percent of

the house sale. He had shown this to her a week earlier, and she was praying about when to tell us.
It was enough to cover the first six months' rent.

Reflection:
1. God had guided and provided for us like only He can do. Does this reassure you that when it's God's idea to do something, He will come through?
2. Remember times He has led you so you can trust Him to do this again.

Fear Arose in My Heart

I sought the Lord, and he answered me; he delivered me from all my fears.
Psalm 34:4

So do not fear, for I am with you; do not be dismayed, for I am your God. I will strengthen you and help you; I will uphold you with my righteous right hand.
Isaiah 41:10

Jay woke me by saying, "Honey, I think you need to take me to the hospital. I think I'm having a heart attack."

My first cry was to God: "NO, don't take him!"

I leapt out of bed and drove him to our local doctor, which was closer than the hospital, a 40-minute drive away. The doctor urgently sent for an ambulance to take Jay straight away. I followed behind in our car. Joshua was six years old and in school. He stayed the night with friends, and I asked everyone I knew to pray.

He went through a series of tests, and they found he had a slightly enlarged aorta. They told me this just as I was leaving to go to bed. Being a nurse, I could only think of the worst-case scenario, as enlarged aortas can suddenly burst.

I stayed in town with some friends. I kept thinking, "I'm going to be a widow at 49 years old with a six-year-old. God, please don't allow this to happen!" I could hardly sleep a wink and couldn't get back to Jay's side quick enough the following day.
The next day, God put a song into my heart from Chris Tomlin: "I Lift My Hands," with repetitive words—Let faith arise. Jay's slightly enlarged aorta was only enlarged by a millimetre. The doctor concluded this was probably normal for him. They requested he return to the hospital in one year.

Reflection:
1. Hearing the news of the bad health of a loved one can be so frightening. What is your immediate response to God?
2. Where is God in the midst of this?

Daily Bears Our Burdens

Praise be to the Lord, to God our Saviour, who daily bears our burdens.
Psalm 68:19

Come to me, all who are weary and burdened, and I will give you rest. . . . For my yoke is easy and my burden is light.
Matthew 11:28, 30

I was packing again. We were to move, as the landlords could not agree on what to do with the house now; they were separating. We had also planned to go back to Canada for two months to see the in-laws. So, to save rent money, we would store our things till we returned.

Out of the blue, the phone rang. It was my brother Peter, who lived with my mother at the

time. "Mary," he said, "Mum was walking across at a pedestrian crossing when a car hit her."

Immediately, I burst into tears, and my ten-year-old son said, "Mum, don't worry, God will take care of this. She will be okay."

New Zealand has three islands: North, South, and Stewart Island. I was living on the South Island, and my mother lived on the North Island. We booked a flight, and I simply left everything. I was on staff at a Bible school and used to plan my days with phone calls, counselling, or business meetings. I had not planned a trip to my mother, but she was now my priority.

I went straight to Mum in intensive care. I announced I was her daughter and was shown directly to her bed. She was very bruised, with a swollen arm, broken ribs, and a bleed on her brain. Doctors couldn't believe she didn't have more broken bones. She was in and out of sleep. I sat with her every day for five days till she went into a ward. Day by day, I had no idea what to expect; yet I felt calm, at peace, and lifted above it all. Friends were praying.

My brother, who lived with my mother, was quite a mess and very anxious for our mother and his future. I needed to sort things out for him as well. Each day, I invited God into this; each day, He carried this burden for me. I got help for my brother, which he needed within a minimal time scale through God's favour.

Reflection:

1. Do you like to be in control of every aspect of your life?
2. Have you experienced God picking up the details of your life when you cannot?

Out of My Control

God is our refuge and strength, an ever-present help in trouble. Therefore we will not fear, though the earth give way and the mountains fall into the heart of the sea.
Psalm 46:1–2

"The city is hit. Buildings down."

What is she talking about? Was that an earthquake? I had just felt the earth roll beneath my feet, but maybe it was because I was 40 km from the city centre, from which this message came.

Ricki was working in the city centre when the Christchurch earthquake struck. She sent the message about the earthquake from Christchurch. I received it on 22 February 2011, at 12.51 pm.

Intuitively, she went under the office desk, both arms bruised from banging from one side to the other. She managed to scramble through, over broken walls of offices and smashed computers; she got down the stairs into her car to drive home. Typically, the drive only took half an hour, but it took two hours to go through cracked streets and around rubble. Her mind was on automatic, trying to escape this disaster as fast as she could, not thinking about aftershocks.

Over 11,000 aftershocks hit the area for weeks following this big one. We had no sense of control over our lives, remaining on high alert, waiting for another earthquake to happen. The sound of a noisy truck rumbling down the road could make your body stiffen, your eyes widen, and your chest tighten. Whether it was an earthquake or not, your immediate reaction was to run outside. Homes, offices, and schools were on high alert: pathways cleared, nothing high above you to fall on you, furniture secured to the walls, coats and bags with essentials ready to evacuate beside the door.

For many of us who liked being in control of our lives, it was hard. We could only look to God for wisdom, protection, and comfort, and remember that God is always there for us.

Reflection:

1. Have you ever experienced a natural disaster like this (in either this country or another one)?

2. We are not to live in dread of bad things happening—like going through an earthquake, or hearing bad news from the doctor, or a death in the family. Instead, we are to trust God cares so much about us, feels our pain, sees our confusion, and loves us enough to walk beside us as we go through it.

Burnout

My flesh and my heart may fail, but God is the strength of my heart and my portion forever.
Psalm 73:26

Surely, I needed to do everything for God because of all He had done for me. My thinking was this: I was not significant; others were. I'm single, so I have the time to give it all.

I had "burnt out" twice, to the point that this extroverted, social girl couldn't see anyone, hear anyone's problems, was physically unable to do much, and slept for hours during the day.

I had read books on how not to burn out, sat in workshops on it, and helped others with it, but I still couldn't see the pattern I seemed to be stuck in until challenged with this simple question—When I say Yes to something, what am I saying No to?

During my years of full-time devotion to God and looking to Him to provide everything, I hurt my husband and my son because I carried on the same crazy lifestyle when I was married as I had when I was single. I seriously believed that this was the right and pleasing thing to do for God. Where did my crazy beliefs come from?

My dear mother's influence played a factor in this. She was selfless, always concerned about others, and generous with her time and any-

thing else she could give; but she had a husband who needed her, so this grounded her to have a better balance in her life than I did then.
God opened my eyes to see what was happening in my life, showing me that He enjoyed it when I took pleasure in things. Slowly, my priorities began to change and return to the order God had intended—God first, family, and then others.
Matthew, a disciple of Jesus, records these words from Jesus: "Take my yoke upon you, and learn from me, for I am gentle and humble in heart, and you will find rest for your souls" (Matthew 11:29).
John, a disciple of Jesus, records these words of Jesus: "The thief comes only to steal and kill and destroy; I have come that they may have life and have it to the full" (John 10:10).

Reflection:
1. Have you experienced burnout?
2. Can you see where the sense of busyness comes from?
3. Before you say Yes to anything else, ask this question—When I say Yes, what am I saying No to?

Honouring Your Parents

Honour your father and your mother, so that you may live long in the land the Lord your God is giving you.
Exodus 20:12

I didn't always get on with my mother. When I was 14 years old, the neighbour came over; she was concerned, as we were arguing loudly. Over the years, God worked on this in my life, and I came to love and respect Mum very much. She was a mighty prayer warrior and loved God.

In 1991, my father died, so she was on her own for a short time until my cousin and then my brother lived with her.

Twelve years later, I returned to New Zealand, now married, so we were physically so much closer to Mum. This continued for ten years. She came and stayed with us three or four times a year. They were such special times.

At 85 years old, my mother had a collision with a car while walking across a zebra crossing. She survived the accident, but it resulted in her losing a lot of confidence and the ability to make wise decisions. At the same time, her house was deteriorating and would need a lot of money spent on it to make it suitable for her to continue living in it. The question arose whether it was time to move her to a local rest home

in a unit. Our time in New Zealand was coming to an end, as our work was calling us back overseas.
A couple in her church looked for a place and found a lovely unit. We prayed Mum's house would sell and the unit they found would still be available. The timing was important as we wanted to help Mum move and see her happily settled before we left the country.
The house was sold. We booked three days to help with the move, and God miraculously organised the timing for it all to come together, from packing up the house, the unit being ready for the move, and us being there to help. Although it was hard to leave her, Mum insisted that we go, and we left knowing she was safe and settled.

Reflection:
1. Do you find it hard to honour your parents? Unfilled and unrealistic expectations can make it hard to respect them.
2. What can we do with the painful memories of our upbringing? Forgiveness takes time; the right thoughts towards them don't come immediately. True forgiveness takes time. First, we need to ask God to forgive them and for God to forgive us for choosing to hold that against them. While we are healing, we can still serve and bless them. Eventually, our feelings will change, and we will feel the difference. Consider these words from Jesus: "Forgive us our debts as we also have forgiven our debtors" (Matthew 6:12).

Abraham Just Went

The Lord had said to Abram, "Go from your country, your people and your father's household to the land I will show you."
Genesis 12:1

Jay and I were seeking God to where we should go next to serve Him. We were living in NZ.

We considered Turkey but then realised we both needed help learning a new language, so it might be best to go to a country where they spoke English.

We were still in a quandary about what to do after corresponding with a few places and needing a clear picture.

A guest speaker in church that Sunday spoke about God leading Abraham. His message showed Jay about going even when he didn't have all the details.

Jay returned home with a new sense of joy and peace and was willing to do this without all the details. I knew this had to be God.

The next day, while we were praying, our seven-year-old son came rushing into the room and asked what we were praying about. We told him we were praying about our future as a family, and with a matter-of-fact attitude, he said, "Mum, if God wants you in England, you'll go there."

So, with few details or even a clear picture of what we would do, we said we were willing to go and booked the tickets to go there. We packed up a four-bedroom house, giving lots away, selling some, storing other things with friends, and settling on six suitcases of everything vital to us to come with us.

Other times when I had left my home country, it was okay, but this was the most challenging move, as I had become attached to certain things, especially our wedding gifts. I couldn't compare this with anything. I thought about all God had done for us through Jesus and the sacrifices He had made. We would trust Him to provide the things we need, and our wants.

And He did. We easily filled a three-bedroom house in England, which overflows with stuff. His faithfulness in guiding us when we surrender our lives to His care and abundance can never disappoint us.

Reflection:

1. Can you see how God was guiding us in this?
2. Can you see God's faithfulness to us?

His Provision Confirms Again

"For I know the plans I have for you," declares the Lord, "plans to prosper you and not to harm you, plans to give you a hope and a future."
Jeremiah 29:11

The situation where we were living changed. We needed to find somewhere to live quite quickly. The estate agent laughed when we told him what we could afford per month. We needed God to make a way where it naturally wouldn't happen.

We asked our friends to pray. Day after day went by, and we waited. God knew our budget and what we needed, and if He wanted us to serve Him in the UK, we needed somewhere to live. We had followed Him here from NZ with much peace and joy as we walked into the unknown.

A friend knew of a minister who had bought a house for their retirement. They weren't ready to retire yet and were happy to rent it out. We had no UK references and no credit here. We met them over tea and then waited for their answer. We had to leave the temporary accommodation by the first of September, and it was now 31 August. At 8 pm, we received an email that we could rent from them at the price we suggested. Now that we had a place to go, we would stay another two weeks until the new place was ready.

God had not only confirmed our place here in the UK, but the landlords also replaced the carpet, freshened by painting the place, and

only required a month's deposit before moving in. (Often six months is needed, especially when you haven't rented in a new city.)
Although it would be a difficult first year with lots of challenges and sometimes tears, God repeatedly confirmed that we were where He wanted us to be.

Reflection:
1. Have you ever panicked about whether God would provide for you?
2. Have you ever needed God to confirm you're still where He wants you to be?

We're in the Same Situation Again

For the Lord God is a sun and shield; the Lord bestows favour and honour; no good thing does he withhold from those whose walk is blameless.
Psalm 84:11

The lovely landlords retired and needed the house we were renting from them. We stored our things and headed to New Zealand to help my dear mother, who seemed to need extra assistance. It would also be our first Christmas home in NZ for several years. We left with no idea where we would live when we returned.

While we were away, we heard of a house that might be available in the community where I was working. We were given temporary accommodation for three weeks, but after that, we could only stay if the owners of the house said we could live there at a rent we could afford.

Three days before leaving the temporary accommodation, we went for a long walk to pray and surrender to God's will for us. As soon as we got back, there was an email from the house owner saying they had accepted our conditions for rent, and we could move in as soon as we needed. God had provided again, even including the answer to my special requests: two toilets, a bath and a shower, a beautiful garden big enough for room for a trampoline for our son, three bedrooms, and most of all, it was in the community of people we loved.

Reflection:

1. Did you ever experience a last-minute miracle?
2. What did you grow in, in this experience?

I Never Saw Them

Whoever is kind to the poor lends to the Lord,
and he will reward them for what they have done.
Proverbs 19:17

My son was ten years old at the time. We were living in the UK. One day, while walking through our town square, he said, "Mum, where is that man going to sleep tonight?"

I hadn't even seen him. He looked like a discarded piece of rubbish pushed to the side of the road. As we drew a little closer, he smelt of stale urine. Who even cared about him? He wasn't my responsibility, but I could see from the look on my son's face that we needed to do something.

"Mum, do we have any food to give him?" I didn't. We decided to buy him a hot beverage and something sweet to eat. Then my son said, "Let's pray he finds somewhere to sleep tonight." My dear son cried as he prayed for him. My heart melted.

I never even noticed or cared enough to connect with such a person. Oh God, forgive me. Who do I think I am? God loves this man. He is someone's son, brother, maybe even a husband or father. I have no idea what led him here. How can I judge him?

Right then, we made a promise, led by my son, to always feed anyone we saw on the street, either from the food we had brought from home or what we could buy. We always agreed to acknowledge "someone

sleeping rough" and say hello, as that was the least we could do for God's precious creation.
God opened my eyes from that day forward.

Reflection:
1. It's always a challenge to make ourselves vulnerable to people different from us, but maybe God wants us to step out of our comfort zone now and then. It is not being gullible but approaching someone with wisdom and allowing them to see God through you in your act of kindness.
2. We cannot judge when we think how, without God, we may have ended up in a similar situation.

Mum Wasn't Mum Anymore

You will keep in perfect peace those whose minds are steadfast, because they trust in you.
Isaiah 26:3

In 2015, my mother forgot my birthday. She had always remembered it. Not long after this, I found out that my mother wasn't well. She had been living in her unit at a retirement complex with a lovely garden and everything she needed, but she had forgotten how to use the microwave, boil a pot of vegetables—and most things to do with the kitchen—and she wasn't eating.

The manager of the residential units where Mum lived encouraged us to come home to New Zealand to assess the situation and decide the next steps. While we were there, Mum saw a doctor, who tested her for Alzheimer's disease. Unfortunately, the report came back that she was in the very early stages of Alzheimer's. Mum could still care for herself in the unit, but an agency sent in help in the form of three visits a day to ensure she was eating and to check on her well-being.

Christmas 2015 was difficult; she would disengage and stare off into nowhere. Watching this extremely intellectual writer struggling to write a sentence on a Christmas card broke my heart.

God, what a cruel disease this was. My mother was mentally disappearing before my eyes; I couldn't get her back. This sharp, witty, bright woman was now dull, distant, and vague.

Why do others still have mothers with working brains? I thought. Then I realised I still had my mother, but I had friends who lost their mothers at 12 years old. I was 52 years old; she'd seen me get married, have my son, been with him for his first six birthdays, and had holidays with us three times a year for ten years. I tried to take comfort in these things, but it all seemed so unfair.

My mother had worried about everything; she thought if she wasn't concerned about something, it meant she didn't care. Now that her mind was going, she was finally at peace. She had nothing to worry about. Someone sat and visited with her, ensuring she had three meals a day and clean clothes. And when she moved into the care home, part of the complex with nurses 24/7, she was safe.

One evening back in England, while praying for her, I gave my mother back into God's safe hands, and I rested in His love and care for her.

Reflection:

1. Changing roles from being the child your parents cared for to now caring for them isn't easy. I never thought my mother would ever really get old, and I certainly never thought she would lose her faculties. For some, this change of roles is a more straightforward journey than for others; but either way, we will need God's help.

God Has a Place for Animals

And God said, "Let the land produce living creatures according to their kinds: the livestock, the creatures that move along the ground, and the wild animals, each according to its kind."
And it was so.
Genesis 1:24

I grew up with cats, getting them as kittens and playing with them for hours. They were great company, easy to maintain, and independent, but could discern when you needed them. They would come around my face as I lay on the bed, upset from a well-deserved telling-off. I could talk to them, tell them things I would never tell anyone else. And I knew whatever I said, it was safe. So, I knew a pet could change anyone's view of life.

Our only child was ten years old. He struggled with school, life in general, and sometimes not wanting to live. God reminded me how pets had always helped me growing up. I knew they could bring him much joy and be a great reason to keep you living.

In one faith, I know cats are like angels and a blessing to the family. Our cat Coco has been that to us. We got him as soon as my husband and son had a residence permit in the UK.

Coco came just when we needed him. God sent him at the right time to our family and soon brought us lots of joy, especially for our son, giving him a reason to get up in the morning.

I began wondering how God feels about animals. I soon found some lovely verses in the holy Scriptures, the Bible, which confirmed what a gift they are to humanity. The story of Noah and the Ark proves God wanted to save the animals. Then, too, there was Jonah 4:11, where God says, "And should I not have concern for the great city of Nineveh, in which there are more than a hundred and twenty thousand people who cannot tell their right hand from their left—and also many animals?" Psalm 104:11–14 and Job 39 also speak of God providing for animals.

Reflection:
1. Have you ever considered God's view of pets and their purpose? For us, Coco, our cat, helped lift my son out of depression and gave him a reason to live. Nothing can replace our daily relationship with God, although He can graciously use animals and people to make life more bearable.

My Experience with Cancer

Truly he is my rock and my salvation; he is my fortress, I will not be shaken.
Psalm 62:6

I had this sore on my upper left arm, about the size of a thumbnail. It broke down and looked quite disgusting, and then it would heal, then repeat the cycle. One day, it bled all over my pillow while I was sleeping. I kept thinking, I must keep knocking this sore on my arm.

Wisely, God had my husband insist I go to sit at the doctor, even without an appointment, and stay until someone would see me. As soon as the doctor saw it, she referred me to a skin cancer clinic to receive immediate attention.

Within two weeks, I was in front of a cancer specialist. It was skin cancer and needed to be cut out. I was to have it removed immediately. [18]

I guess it's the word cancer and the unknown of "what kind of cancer" that threw my head in a spin. Plus, I was annoyed at myself that I had not gone for help sooner.

My mind went through all the scenarios. What if I lose my arm? What if it's one of those nasty skin cancers, and it's spread throughout my body? Shall I tell my son what I'm going through or wait for the results? I don't want to scare him unnecessarily. Hubby is scared, and I must be strong until we get the results. God, why would you let this happen to me?

Reflection:

1. Questions are okay. We wouldn't be very typical if we didn't have them. David in the Bible had lots of questions for God. The Psalms are full of them.
2. Step by step, where was God in this?
3. Fears of the unknown are usual. Where do you go with your questions?

[18] In the end· the cancer didn't spread throughout my body; it just needed two operations to get it fully out·

I Looked Out the Window

My help comes from the Lord, the Maker of heaven and earth. He will not let your foot slip—he who watches over you will not slumber.
Psalm 121:2–3

Where was that smoke coming from? Oh no, something is not right out there next to our house.

I was working from home and struggling to stay awake. I was still recovering from myocarditis, so I was still having two naps a day. Adjusting to the medication and building up strength was taking time.

Suddenly, I noticed a lot of smoke. The neighbours were having an extension added to their home, and the builders always had a cigarette in their mouths. At first, I thought it must just be one of them smoking near our fence, but there was a lot of smoke. Leaning over my desk and looking intently down through our window, I saw large flames as the wooden fence between the neighbour's yard and ours caught fire.

I yelled out for Jay, who was at the front of the house. Immediately, he went downstairs and outside. Calling the builders over, together with buckets of water, they put the fire out.

One of the builders was using a machine that let off sparks. It was summer, so the bush around the fence was extremely dry and caught alight. God himself did not sleep and kept me awake, so I saw the fire, saving our home from burning down.

Reflection:

1. Can you see how God is alive and active in our day? How can He provide ways to help us when we don't even know we need help?
2. Can you trust Him to keep our eyes open and guide us as needed?

Remember Who You Are Asking to Do This

Then the word of the Lord came to Jeremiah: "I am the Lord, the God of all mankind; Is anything too hard for me?"
Jeremiah 32:26–27

2020 was a very different year for most of us around the world. For me, this was a year that changed my life in unexpected ways.

My heart message is for people to see and experience God as the big and yet personal God that He is, so I thought I should start recording stories for our son. He was born when I was almost 43, and he knew nothing of my first 40 years of life.

At the same time, I came across a group called Writers Learning Together on Facebook and decided to check it out. I felt a bit of a fraud, as I wasn't an author and had no idea what I was doing. They listened to my stories and encouraged me. Surprisingly, I began to enjoy writing and didn't want to stop. At this point, I only wanted to write stories for our son.

Through this group, I discovered webinars to learn more about this craft. I decided to go, again thinking this was a bit embarrassing as I didn't belong here.

Some friends offered to pray with people about the future. I signed up for a Zoom prayer encounter. Without knowing what I was pursuing, one lady said, "I believe God wants you to write a book, and it's for more people than you think."

Back in my bedroom after the prayer meeting, I reminded God of my struggles with education, being dyslexic, not being able to spell, teachers thinking I wouldn't amount to much . . . and instead, I felt a deep joy and peace that I was to do this.

In the summer of 2021, we were allowed out after the lockdowns, so I went to friends in Derby for a week and couldn't stop writing. God was reminding me of stories, downloading them in the day and night. I filled out an A4 journal and was so happy.

In 2022, itching to keep learning and writing more, I heard of an Author Training School, applied, accepted, and never looked back.

It's been quite a journey from the girl in my first story in this book to who I am now.

Reflection:

1. Through this story and most of them in this book, can you see how God can take an ordinary person and work through them to bless others?

2. With God, there are no limitations. Simply be willing and available and go on one fantastic venture with Him.